Collins

T0337298

COBUILD
Key Words for
Insurance

HarperCollins Publishers
Westerhill Road
Bishopbriggs
Glasgow
G64 2QT

First Edition 2013

Reprint 10 9 8 7 6 5 4 3 2 1 0

© HarperCollins Publishers 2013

ISBN 978-0-00-748983-1

Collins® and COBUILD® are
registered trademarks of
HarperCollins Publishers Limited

www.collinselt.com
www.collinsdictionary.com/cobuild

A catalogue record for this book is
available from the British Library

Audio recorded by Networks SRL,
Milan, Italy

Acknowledgements
We would like to thank those
authors and publishers who kindly
gave permission for copyright
material to be used in the Collins
Corpus. We would also like to thank
Times Newspapers Ltd for providing
valuable data.

Contents

Contributors

Specialist consultants
Mariette Knoblauch, Chartered Professional Accountant,
Ballard Beancounters, Seattle USA

Mike Seymour, author of *Hotel and Hospitality English*
and *English for Insurance Professionals*, and contributor
to German EFL magazine *Business Spotlight*

Project manager
Patrick White

Editors
Katherine Carroll
Kate Mohideen
Enid Pearsons
Elizabeth Walter
Kate Woodford

Computing support
Mark Taylor

For the publisher
Gerry Breslin
Lucy Cooper
Kerry Ferguson
Gavin Gray
Elaine Higgleton
Persephone Lock
Ruth O'Donovan
Rosie Pearce
Lisa Sutherland

Introduction

Collins COBUILD Key Words for Insurance is a brand-new vocabulary book for students who want to master the English of Insurance in order to study or work in the field. This title contains the 500 most important English words and phrases relating to Insurance, as well as a range of additional features which have been specially designed to help you to *really* understand and use the language of this specific area.

The main body of the book contains alphabetically organized dictionary-style entries for the key words and phrases of Insurance. These vocabulary items have been specially chosen to fully prepare you for the type of language that you will need in this field. Many are specialized terms that are very specific to this profession and area of study. Others are more common or general words and phrases that are often used in the context of Insurance.

Each word and phrase is explained clearly and precisely, in English that is easy to understand. In addition, each entry is illustrated with examples taken from the Collins Corpus. Of course, you will also find grammatical information about the way that the words and phrases behave.

In amongst the alphabetically organized entries, you will find valuable word-building features that will help you gain a better understanding of this area of English. For example, some features provide extra help with tricky pronunciations, while others pull together groups of related words that can usefully be learned as a set.

At the start of this book you will see lists of words and phrases, helpfully organized by topic area. You can use these lists to revise sets of vocabulary and to prepare for writing tasks. You can also download the audio for this book from www.collinselt.com/audio. This contains a recording of each headword in the book, followed by an example sentence. This will help you to learn and remember pronunciations of words and phrases. Furthermore, the exercise section at the end of this book gives you an opportunity to memorize important words and phrases, to assess what you have learned, and to work out which areas still need attention.

So whether you are studying Insurance, or you are already working in the field and intend to improve your career prospects, we are confident that *Collins COBUILD Key Words for Insurance* will equip you for success in the future.

Guide to Dictionary Entries

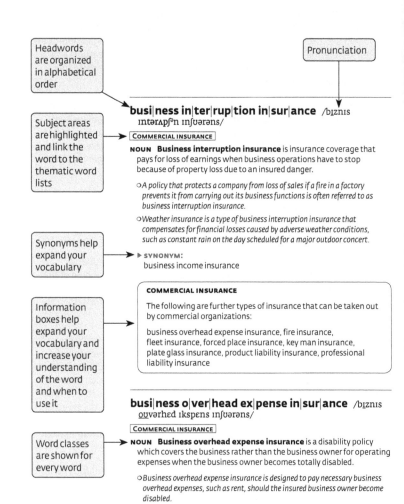

Headwords are organized in alphabetical order

Pronunciation

Subject areas are highlighted and link the word to the thematic word lists

Synonyms help expand your vocabulary

Information boxes help expand your vocabulary and increase your understanding of the word and when to use it

Word classes are shown for every word

busi|ness in|ter|rup|tion in|sur|ance /bɪznɪs ɪntərʌpʃªn ɪnʃʊərəns/

COMMERCIAL INSURANCE

NOUN **Business interruption insurance** is insurance coverage that pays for loss of earnings when business operations have to stop because of property loss due to an insured danger.

○ A policy that protects a company from loss of sales if a fire in a factory prevents it from carrying out its business functions is often referred to as business interruption insurance.

○ Weather insurance is a type of business interruption insurance that compensates for financial losses caused by adverse weather conditions, such as constant rain on the day scheduled for a major outdoor concert.

▶ **SYNONYM:**
business income insurance

COMMERCIAL INSURANCE

The following are further types of insurance that can be taken out by commercial organizations:

business overhead expense insurance, fire insurance, fleet insurance, forced place insurance, key man insurance, plate glass insurance, product liability insurance, professional liability insurance

---

busi|ness o|ver|head ex|pense in|sur|ance /bɪznɪs ouvərhɛd ɪkspɛns ɪnʃʊərəns/

COMMERCIAL INSURANCE

NOUN **Business overhead expense insurance** is a disability policy which covers the business rather than the business owner for operating expenses when the business owner becomes totally disabled.

○ Business overhead expense insurance is designed to pay necessary business overhead expenses, such as rent, should the insured business owner become disabled.

○ Business overhead expense insurance is disability insurance that steps in and pays the business expenses of a business owner while he is disabled.

Guide to Dictionary Entries

CO|BRA /ˈkoʊbrə/ (short for **Consolidated Omnibus Budget Reconciliation Act**)

MEDICAL INSURANCE

ABBREVIATION In the U.S., **COBRA** insurance provides continuation of group health coverage insurance after an employee may have lost health insurance benefits at the end of employment.

○When you stop working for an employer, they will probably offer you COBRA medical coverage.

○When coverage ends, you will be offered the option of extending coverage under COBRA.

a|ban|don /əˈbændən/ (**abandons, abandoned, abandoning**)

CLAIMS

VERB If you **abandon** insured property that has suffered partial loss or damage, you give it to the insurers so that a claim for a total loss may be made.

○Under such conditions, the ocean marine policy permits the insured to abandon the damaged ship or cargo to the insurer and make a claim for the entire value.

○The insured may claim for a partial loss or abandon the property to the insurance company and claim a total loss.

▶ COLLOCATIONS:
abandon a property
abandon a ship
abandon a vehicle

Variants of the headword, such as abbreviated, full forms and British forms, are also shown

Definitions explain what the word means in simple language

Examples show how the word is used in context

All the different forms of the word are listed

Collocations help you put the word into practice

Guide to Pronunciation Symbols

Vowel Sounds

ɑ	calm, ah
ɑr	heart, far
æ	act, mass
aɪ	dive, cry
aɪər	fire, tire
aʊ	out, down
aʊər	flour, sour
ɛ	met, lend, pen
eɪ	say, weight
ɛər	fair, care
ɪ	fit, win
i	feed, me
ɪər	near, beard
ɒ	lot, spot
oʊ	note, coat
ɔ	claw, bought
ɔr	more, cord
ɔɪ	boy, joint
ʊ	could, stood
u	you, use
ʊər	lure, endure
ɜr	turn, third
ʌ	fund, must
ə	*the first vowel in* about
ər	*the first vowel in* forgotten
i	*the second vowel in* very
u	*the second vowel in* actual

Consonant Sounds

b	bed, rub
d	done, red
f	fit, if
g	good, dog
h	hat, horse
y	yellow, you
k	king, pick
l	lip, bill
ᵊl	handle, panel
m	mat, ram
n	not, tin
ᵊn	hidden, written
p	pay, lip
r	run, read
s	soon, bus
t	talk, bet
v	van, love
w	win, wool
ʍ	why, wheat
z	zoo, buzz
ʃ	ship, wish
ʒ	measure, leisure
ŋ	sing, working
tʃ	cheap, witch
θ	thin, myth
ð	then, other
dʒ	joy, bridge

Word Lists

CLAIMS
abandon
adjust
adjusted
appraiser
claim
claimant
claim form
claims investigator
claims notification
claims ratio
combined ratio
consequential loss
deny a claim
file a claim
leakage
long-term care insurance
loss adjuster
pay a claim
payout
pay out
recovery
retention
settle a claim
subrogation
total loss

COMMERCIAL INSURANCE
all-risk policy
ambulance insurance
arson
arsonist
average adjuster
aviation insurance
binder
bonded
bonding
book of business
business interruption insurance
business overhead expense
insurance
civil unrest
credit card insurance
deductible
estimated maximum loss
excess
fire insurance
fleet insurance
fleet rate
forced place insurance
force majeure

franchise
hurricane
key man insurance
loss
marine insurance
mortgage insurance
natural catastrophe
open policy
plate glass insurance
product liability insurance
professional liability insurance
riot
salvage
umbrella policy

Marine insurance
general average
ocean marine insurance
salvage

GENERAL
accident insurance
cancel a policy
captive
casualty
contingency
cover
coverage
damage
D&O insurance
defraud
expiration date
expire
fraud
fraudulent
front-end load
gatekeeper
general insurance
hazard
high-risk
indemnity
institution
insurability
insurable
insurable interest
insurance
insurance class
insure
insured
insurer
IRS

issue a policy
legal expenses insurance
liability
liable
line of business
Lloyd's of London
loss ratio
manage a risk
mitigate a risk
moral hazard
mutual
mutual fund
mutual insurance
mutual insurer
NAIC
negligence
negligent
overinsured
personal injury
personal injury insurance
personal liability insurance
plan
PMI
policy
policyholder
policy issuance
policy term
policy wording
portability
portfolio
premium
premium income
promissory
proof of coverage
property and casualty insurance
provision
rebate
reduce a risk
regular premium
reimburse
reimbursement
renew
renewal
renewal date
report a claim
report an accident
rescind a contract
rescission
reserves
residual
residual debt insurance

retain
risk
risk management
risk manager
risk pooling
run-off
schedule
self-insurance
service industry
severe
severity
short-tail business
supplementary insurance
take out insurance
terms and conditions
third party
third party liability
travel insurance
underinsured
unemployment insurance
uninsurable
uninsured
utmost good faith
valued policy
void

LIFE INSURANCE
actuarial science
actuary
AD&D
appointed actuary
assets
assign a policy
back-end load
beneficiary
benefit
benefits
bodily injury
bonus
contributory
convertible term insurance
death benefits
deceased
decreasing term insurance
deferred annuity
dependent
dividend
double indemnity
dynamic insurance
early retirement
endowment insurance

endowment mortgage
endowment policy
equity-linked policy
escalation
estate
experience table
funeral
funeral expenses
funeral plan
group insurance
immediate annuity
inception
index
investment bond
level premium term insurance
life insurance
life table
longevity risk
long-tail claims
lump sum payment
make a policy paid up
mature
maturity
maturity value
morbidity table
mortality rate
mortality table
no-load
noncontributory
nonparticipating
paid-up
participating
participating insurance
policy loan
provision
renewable term insurance
reversion
reversionary bonus
second-hand endowment
single life annuity
single premium
single premium insurance
spouse
sum assured
surrender
surrender value
survive
surviving
term insurance
tontine
traded endowment

traditional policy
variable universal life insurance
viatical settlement
waiting period
whole life insurance
widow
widower
will
workers' compensation

Pensions
401K
annuitant
annuitize
annuity
annuity rate
commutation
commute
contribution
CPI
defined benefit plan
defined contribution plan
draw a pension
index-linked
inflation rider
joint life annuity
pay a pension
retire
retiree
retirement
retirement age
standard annuity
tracker fund
trust
trustee

MEDICAL INSURANCE
ability to work
ADL
any occupation
cash plan
catastrophic illness
COBRA
copay
critical illness insurance
deferred period
dental care
dental insurance
disability clause
disability insurance

disorder
eligibility
eligible
emergency room
employer-provided
FSA
health insurance exchange
health maintenance organization
health maintenance plan
health questionnaire
high-deductible health plan
HIPAA
HRA
HSA
impairment
income protection insurance
indemnity plan
inpatient
lifetime limit
longevity
maximum lifetime benefit
Medicaid
medical procedure
medical underwriting
Medicare
Medigap policy
Medivac
mental impairment
mutual aid society
on-the-job injury
operation
outpatient
own occupation coverage
own or similar occupation
physical impairment
physician
PMI
PPACA
preexisting condition
preferred provider organization
preferred provider plan
private health insurance
repatriate
repatriation
repatriation expenses
terminal illness
vision care
waiver of premium

REINSURANCE
bordereau

catastrophe excess of loss
cedant
cede
coinsurance
coinsure
coinsurer
contribution
excess of loss reinsurance
facultative
first-loss policy
nonproportional cover
pool a risk
primary insurer
probable maximum loss
proportional reinsurance coverage
quota share reinsurance
reinsurance
reinsurance treaty
reinsure
reinsurer
retention of risk
retrocession
risk excess of loss
stop loss reinsurance
surplus reinsurance
treaty

RESIDENCE INSURANCE
actual cash value basis
condominium
condo owner
depreciate
depreciation
earthquake
earthquake coverage
fire extinguisher
floater
flood
flood coverage
home insurance
homeowner
landslide
lightning
malicious damage
possessions
property
real estate
real estate insurance
real estate liability
renter
renter's insurance

replacement cost basis
replacement cost insurance
residence insurance
safety device
subsidence
sum insured
tenant
theft
tornado
tsunami

SALES AND DISTRIBUTION
acquisition costs
agency
brokerage
churn
commission
cooling-off period
direct insurer
distribution channel
financial adviser
gross premium
gross written premiums
initial commission
insurance agent
insurance broker
insurance salesman
intermediary
lapse
new business
new business profit margin
proposal
proposal form
proposer
quote
reviewable
shop around
trail commission
upfront

UNDERWRITING
accept a risk
act of God
adverse selection
assumption of risk
biometric risk
calculate a premium
calculate a risk
disclose
disclosure
E&O

endorse
endorsement
exclude a risk
exclusion
experience rating
exposed to
exposure
financial underwriter
financial underwriting
gender
line
load
loading
low-risk
non-disclosure
occupation
occupational group
occupational hazard
partial
particular average
peril
refuse a proposal
rider
syndicate
technical reserves
total probable loss
underwrite
underwriter
underwriting
write cover

VEHICLE INSURANCE
accident-free discount
automobile insurance
collide with
collision coverage
collision damage waiver
comprehensive
crash
fender-bender
GAP insurance
good driver discount
hit and run
MVA
no-fault insurance
safety belt
vehicle
vehicle insurance
write off
write-off

A–Z

Aa

4|0|1|K /fɔr oʊ wʌn keɪ/ (**401Ks**)

LIFE INSURANCE: PENSIONS

NOUN A **401K** is a U.S. retirement saving scheme. Named for subsection 401(k) of the U.S. Internal Revenue code.

○ *401K plans are part of a group of retirement plans known as defined contribution plans.*

○ *If your employer offers a 401K, and you participate in it as soon as possible, you can have a sizable amount in your account by the time you retire.*

---

a|ban|don /əbændən/ (**abandons, abandoned, abandoning**)

CLAIMS

VERB If you **abandon** insured property that has suffered partial loss or damage, you give it to the insurers so that a claim for a total loss may be made.

○ *Under such conditions, the ocean marine policy permits the insured to abandon the damaged ship or cargo to the insurer and make a claim for the entire value.*

○ *The insured may claim for a partial loss or abandon the property to the insurance company and claim a total loss.*

▶ **COLLOCATIONS:**
abandon a property
abandon a ship
abandon a vehicle

---

a|bil|i|ty to work /əbɪlɪti tu wɜrk/

MEDICAL INSURANCE

NOUN A policyholder's **ability to work** is the degree to which they are able to do a job, as a result of disability.

○ A serious illness or injury can harm more than your health – it can have an impact on your ability to work and meet your family's living expenses.

○ Under functional impairment benefits, payouts are made irrespective of the client's ability to work.

---

ac|cept a risk /ˈæksɛpt ə rɪsk/ (accepts a risk, accepted a risk, accepting a risk)

UNDERWRITING

PHRASE If an insurance company **accepts a risk**, it agrees to underwrite a risk or to accept a person or company as a client.

○ An underwriter is a person who decides whether to accept a risk and calculates the premium to be charged.

○ Proposers have a duty to disclose to the insurance company anything that they know which could affect the decision of the insurance company to accept the risk of insurance.

---

ac|ci|dent-free dis|count (ABBR AFD) /ˈæksɪdənt fri dɪskaʊnt/ (accident-free discounts)

VEHICLE INSURANCE

NOUN An **accident-free discount** is a discount on insurance payments that is available to drivers who have no accidents where they are at fault over a particular period of time.

○ If you haven't had an accident in a while, be sure to ask your agent if you qualify for an accident-free discount.

○ After three years with no at-fault accidents, you receive an accident-free discount on your premium.

---

ac|ci|dent in|sur|ance /ˈæksɪdənt ɪnʃʊərəns/

GENERAL

NOUN **Accident insurance** is insurance that provides compensation for accidental injury or death.

○ Aviation insurance is aircraft insurance that includes coverage of aircraft or their contents, the owner's liability, and accident insurance on the passengers.

○ Accident insurance covers death, dismemberment, loss of sight, loss of income, and medical expenses caused by accidental injury.

ac|qui|si|tion costs /ækwɪzɪʃ°n kɔsts/

SALES AND DISTRIBUTION

NOUN Acquisition costs are the total costs of writing or issuing an insurance policy.

○ Surrender values vary greatly, and may be poor in the first years before the insurance company has recouped its acquisition costs from the policy.

○ Acquisition costs include selling expenses, such as advertising, risk classification, commissions, preparing of policies, and recording data.

act of God /ækt əv gɒd/ (acts of God)

UNDERWRITING

NOUN An act of God is an accident or event that happens due to natural causes, such as a storm, earthquake, etc.

○ Suggesting that an event was an act of God may be a defense in English law against a claim for liability since it may be held that it could not have been foreseen or safeguarded against.

○ Hurricanes, earthquakes, and floods are considered as acts of God, as they are natural occurrences beyond human control or influence.

ac|tu|al cash val|ue ba|sis /æktʃuəl kæʃ vælyu beɪsɪs/

RESIDENCE INSURANCE

NOUN Actual cash value basis is a method of valuing insured property that is calculated by subtracting depreciation from the replacement cost.

○ Coverage can be written on a replacement basis or an actual cash value basis that makes an adjustment for depreciation.

○ Contents losses are always adjusted on an actual cash value basis to allow for reduction in the value of the insured items.

ac|tu|ar|i|al sci|ence /æktʃuɛəriəl saɪəns/

LIFE INSURANCE

NOUN Actuarial science is a specialist branch of mathematics applying the laws of statistics and probability to insurance.

○ Insurers use actuarial science to quantify the risks they are willing to assume and the premium they will charge to assume them.

A

○ *The actuarial science of price-setting of policies uses statistics and probability to approximate the rate of future claims based on a given risk.*

▶ **SYNONYM:**
actuarial mathematics

---

ac|tu|ar|y /ækt∫uɛri/ (**actuaries**)

LIFE INSURANCE

NOUN An **actuary** is a mathematician who uses statistics to calculate premiums, dividends, or pension, insurance and annuity rates for an insurance company.

○ *An actuary makes calculations to decide the amount that needs to be contributed into the plan to ensure the target retirement income goal is reached.*

○ *Actuaries assemble and analyze data to estimate the probability and likely cost of the occurrence of an event such as death, sickness, injury, disability, or loss of property.*

A|D|&|D /eɪ di ən di/

LIFE INSURANCE

ABBREVIATION In the U.S., **AD&D** is a type of insurance that provides payment if an accident causes death or loss of a limb, eyesight, or hearing.

○ *An AD&D policy pays a benefit for death, loss of use of limbs, loss of speech, loss of hearing, or loss of sight as the direct result of an accident.*

○ *Under the AD&D provision, the coverage is doubled in the event of an accidental death.*

---

ad|just /ədʒʌst/ (**adjusts, adjusted, adjusting**)

CLAIMS

VERB If you **adjust** a claim, you decide the amount that needs to be paid in order to settle it.

○ *Adjusting flood insurance claims can be a very difficult and trying process.*

○ *In employer group health insurance plans, the premium or the rate may be adjusted annually depending on the loss experience.*

▶ **COLLOCATIONS:**
adjust a claim
adjust a premium

ad|just|ed /ədʒʌstɪd/

CLAIMS

ADJECTIVE An **adjusted** claim has been evaluated by a loss adjuster to decide how much the insurer should pay to the person making the claim.

○ *After negotiation with the claimant, a check or draft is issued for the amount of the adjusted claim.*

○ *The contract contains a provision that the final adjusted premium may not be less than a stated amount.*

A|D|L /eɪ di ɛl/ (short for **activities of daily living**)

MEDICAL INSURANCE

ABBREVIATION ADL are activities such as washing, dressing, and shopping that people must be able to do in order to be considered independent.

○ *The policy provides home and community-based coverage for all persons with two or more ADL impairments.*

○ *The contract defines chronically ill as being unable to perform two of the six ADLs for at least 90 days.*

PRONUNCIATION

Three-letter abbreviations are usually pronounced as separate letters with the main stress on the last syllable.
ADL /eɪ di ɛl/
HRA /eitʃ ɑr eɪ/
IRS /aɪ ɑr ɛs/
PMI /pi ɛm aɪ/

---

ad|verse se|lec|tion /ædvɜrs sɪlɛkʃⁿn/

UNDERWRITING

NOUN **Adverse selection** is a term used to describe the tendency of those in dangerous jobs or with high-risk lifestyles to want to take out life insurance.

○ *Insurance companies need to limit the risk of adverse selection, and ensure that not only the "bad" risks seek insurance.*

○ *Since there is a tendency for those most likely to have losses to take out health insurance, an element of adverse selection exists.*

A

a|gen|cy /ˈeɪdʒənsi/ (agencies)

<u>SALES AND DISTRIBUTION</u>

NOUN An **agency** is a group of people who sell and manage insurance contracts.

- ○ As an independent insurance agency, we help you find insurance solutions tailored to your individual needs.
- ○ We are an independent agency with many insurance carriers offering quality auto insurance coverage.

all-risk pol|i|cy /ɔːl rɪsk pɒlɪsi/ (all-risk policies)

<u>COMMERCIAL INSURANCE</u>

NOUN An **all-risk policy** is an insurance policy that covers all loss or damage however it is caused, apart from any stated exceptions.

- ○ A named-peril policy covers the policyholder only for the risks named in the policy in contrast to an all-risk policy, which covers all causes of loss except those specifically excluded.
- ○ An all-risk policy is different from a peril-specific policy that covers losses from only those perils listed in the policy.

am|bu|lance in|sur|ance /æmbyələns ɪnʃʊərəns/

<u>COMMERCIAL INSURANCE</u>

NOUN **Ambulance insurance** is insurance cover that covers the cost of an emergency ambulance if one is needed.

- ○ Air ambulance insurance provides coverage in the event of a medical emergency which requires air ambulance transport.
- ○ Many low-cost forms of health insurance omit ambulance insurance, so that, while an ambulance will still respond to your emergency call, you'll be entirely without insurance to cover its costs.

an|nu|i|tant /ənuːɪtənt/ (annuitants)

<u>LIFE INSURANCE: PENSIONS</u>

NOUN An **annuitant** is a person receiving an income under an annuity contract.

- ○ The annuity starts making regular payments to the annuitant within a year.
- ○ Life annuity payments, once begun, continue throughout the remaining lifetime of the annuitant, but not beyond.

an|nu|i|tize /ənuːɪtaɪz/ (**annuitizes, annuitized, annuitizing**)

LIFE INSURANCE: PENSIONS

VERB If you **annuitize** a lump sum payment, you convert it into a regular income such as a pension or annuity.

○ *Retirees should annuitize a portion of their nest egg at retirement, in order to provide a guaranteed, inflation-adjusted supplement to their social security.*

○ *On retirement, if you annuitize your account, the insurance company makes a payment on a regular basis for as long as you live.*

an|nu|i|ty /ənuːɪti/ (**annuities**)

LIFE INSURANCE: PENSIONS

NOUN An **annuity** is a contract of insurance to provide an income to the policyholder for a set period of time.

○ *Deferred annuities allow assets to grow tax-deferred over time before being converted to payments to the annuitant.*

○ *The fixed annuity guarantees the principal and provides a lifetime income after retirement.*

an|nu|i|ty rate /ənuːɪti reɪt/ (**annuity rates**)

LIFE INSURANCE: PENSIONS

NOUN An **annuity rate** is used to calculate the amount of income that will be paid, following investment of a lump sum in an annuity.

○ *With a guaranteed annuity rate written into your pension contract, your provider must offer that minimum annuity income to you on retirement.*

○ *If a guaranteed annuity rate is applied to the total cash proceeds available from a policy, then one of the biggest risks is the equity market shooting up.*

an|y oc|cu|pa|tion /ɛni ɒkyəpeɪʃ°n/

MEDICAL INSURANCE

PHRASE **Any occupation** insurance covers a person if they cannot work under any circumstances, in any occupation, following an accident, injury, or disability.

○ *Insured policyholders are considered totally disabled only if their disabilities prevent them from working at any occupation for which they are reasonably suited by education, training, or experience.*

○ *One company may consider you disabled if you're unable to work in any occupation, while another may require only that you're unable to work in your current occupation.*

▶ **SYNONYM:**
any job

---

ap|point|ed ac|tu|ar|y /əpɔɪntɪd æktʃuɛri/ (**appointed actuaries**)

LIFE INSURANCE

NOUN An **appointed actuary** is an actuary appointed by a life insurance company, whose main role is to carry out a regular valuation of the reserves held to pay future policy benefits.

○ *The proposed revisions required an appointed actuary to produce a report attesting to the fact that a company had booked reserves satisfying the minimum reserve requirements.*

○ *The appointed actuary is required to produce a report attesting to the fact that a company has created reserves satisfying the minimum reserve requirements.*

---

ap|prais|er /əpreɪzər/ (**appraisers**)

CLAIMS

NOUN An **appraiser** is an expert in the valuation of certain types of property, who provides expert advice to insurance loss adjusters.

○ *During an appraisal process, appraisers need not view each piece of damaged personal property in calculating the amount of the loss.*

○ *The appraisers will separately state the actual cash value, the replacement cost, and the amount of loss to each item.*

▶ **SYNONYM:**
assessor

---

ar|son /ɑrsən/

COMMERCIAL INSURANCE

NOUN **Arson** is the crime of deliberately setting fire to something, especially a building.

○ *A Fire Marshall is a public official involved in fire prevention and in investigation of fires particularly where arson is suspected.*

○ *Evidence of possible arson by the insureds provided a good reason to deny their fire claim.*

---

ar|son|ist /ˈɑrsənɪst/ (**arsonists**)

COMMERCIAL INSURANCE

NOUN An **arsonist** is a person who commits the crime of arson.

○ *Evidence suggested the blaze could be the work of arsonists.*

○ *The declaration states that an arsonist set fire to the insured's home, and the fire was extinguished one day later.*

---

as|sets /ˈæsɛts/

LIFE INSURANCE

NOUN **Assets** are items that are owned by an individual, such as property and investments.

○ *The balance sheet shows assets, including investments and reinsurance, and liabilities, such as loss reserves to pay claims in the future.*

○ *Insurance does not protect the assets but only compensates the policyholder for economic or financial loss.*

---

as|sign a pol|i|cy /əˈsaɪn ə ˈpɒlɪsi/ (**assigns a policy, assigned a policy, assigning a policy**)

LIFE INSURANCE

PHRASE If you **assign a policy**, you transfer legal ownership of an insurance policy to another person.

○ *The policy may be assigned to someone else by written request of the current owner.*

○ *Since a whole life policy has a cash value component, it may be considered an asset; but assigning the policy to a trust means that it can no longer be considered an asset for that individual.*

---

as|sump|tion of risk /əˈsʌmpʃ³n əv ˈrɪsk/

UNDERWRITING

NOUN **Assumption of risk** is the practice of paying for minor losses yourself, but protecting against catastrophic losses by buying insurance cover.

A

- ○ *Under the assumption of risk doctrine, a person who understands and recognizes the danger inherent in a particular activity cannot recover damages in the event of injury.*
- ○ *The courts held that assumption of risk meant that workers assumed liability for accidents caused by risks common to employment.*

▶ **SYNONYM:**
risk assumption

---

au|to|mo|bile in|sur|ance (INFORMAL **auto insurance**)
/ˈɔtəməbɪl ɪnʃʊərəns/

VEHICLE INSURANCE

NOUN **Automobile insurance** is insurance coverage for cars.

- ○ *Your personal automobile insurance may already cover you for damage to a rental car.*
- ○ *If you are involved in an accident while operating a personally owned vehicle or a vehicle leased in your name, liability protection will be governed by your automobile insurance coverage.*

---

av|er|age ad|just|er /ˈævərɪdʒ ədʒʌstər/ (**average adjusters**)

COMMERCIAL INSURANCE

NOUN An **average adjuster** is a person who calculates average claims, especially for marine insurance.

- ○ *An average adjuster is a marine claims specialist responsible for adjusting and providing the general average statement.*
- ○ *An average bond guarantees that a cargo owner will pay his or her contribution to the general average loss, once it has been determined by the average adjuster.*

---

a|vi|a|tion in|sur|ance /eɪvieɪʃən ɪnʃʊərəns/

COMMERCIAL INSURANCE

NOUN **Aviation insurance** is insurance cover for aircraft, and for damage, injury, or loss of life or cargo while traveling on aircraft.

- ○ *A number of countries require aviation insurance for accident and sickness on airline passengers and crews.*
- ○ *Aviation insurance will cover accident and liability risks, as well as hull damage, connected with the operation of aircraft.*

Bb

---

back-end load /bæk ɛnd loʊd/ (back-end loads)

LIFE INSURANCE

NOUN A **back-end load** is a charge that an investor pays when they cancel a life insurance policy.

○ *Universal life policies usually carry a back-end load, often called a surrender charge, which ordinarily is a graded penalty applied against the cash value if the policy is terminated within a few years of issue.*

○ *When the investor exits a mutual fund, a back-end load is applied which reduces the redemption value.*

---

ben|e|fi|ciar|y /bɛnɪfɪʃiɛri/ (beneficiaries)

LIFE INSURANCE

NOUN A **beneficiary** of a life insurance policy is the person who receives the proceeds, often the widow or widower of the insured.

○ *The policy provides either a stated sum or a periodic income to your designated beneficiaries upon your death.*

○ *If death occurs within 10 years after the annuity payments begin, payments are continued to a named beneficiary for the remainder of the 10 years.*

▶ **COLLOCATION:**
  beneficiary of

---

ben|e|fit /bɛnɪfɪt/ (benefits, benefited, benefiting)

LIFE INSURANCE

VERB If you **benefit from** an insurance policy, then the policy will pay you money if a particular event, such as the death of a relative, occurs.

○ *Unlike with medical insurance, the policyholder himself doesn't benefit from life insurance; it is his nominee who receives a payout upon the untimely death of the policyholder.*

B

○One danger of self-employment can be that you tend not to benefit from insurance coverage coming from a company.

▶ COLLOCATION:
benefit from

---

ben|e|fits /bɛnɪfɪts/

LIFE INSURANCE

NOUN The **benefits** of a life or medical insurance policy are the money that it pays out.

○The extra hazard generally requires an extra premium rating or waiver of certain benefits or coverage.

○Medical Expense Insurance provides benefits for expenses incurred for medical care.

---

bind|er /baɪndər/ (binders)

COMMERCIAL INSURANCE

NOUN A **binder** is an informal agreement that gives insurance coverage while you are waiting for a policy to be formally issued.

○A binder is given to an applicant for insurance during the time it takes an insurance company to complete the policy paperwork.

○As a general rule, coverage does not begin until a policy is issued by the insurer, unless the insurer's agent issues a binder.

---

bi|o|met|ric risk /baɪəmɛtrɪk rɪsk/ (biometric risks)

UNDERWRITING

NOUN **Biometric risk** covers all risks related to human life conditions, such as death, birth, disability, age, and number of children.

○If the institution offering the pension scheme underwrites the liability to cover against biometric risk, they must hold on a permanent basis additional assets above the technical provisions to serve as a buffer.

○More usually, insurance is sought in the face of adverse outcomes such as bad health or loss due to theft or damage, whereas biometric risk involves the risk that the individual lives to or beyond a certain age.

bod|i|ly in|ju|ry /bɒdɪli ɪndʒəri/ (bodily injuries)

LIFE INSURANCE

NOUN The **bodily injury** section of a liability insurance policy usually covers hospital bills for the injured parties as well as related expenses such as rehabilitation, medicines, and lost income.

○ *There is optional coverage under an auto policy to pay for medical expenses for bodily injury caused by an auto accident, regardless of fault.*

○ *The court ruled that his conduct did create a substantial risk of death or serious bodily injury.*

---

bond|ed /bɒndɪd/

COMMERCIAL INSURANCE

ADJECTIVE If your employees are **bonded**, you are insured against theft, damage, or embezzlement carried out by them while they are working for you.

○ *The insurance company will pay the insured business or individual for money or other property lost because of dishonest acts of its bonded employees.*

○ *All workers are bonded, so you will not be liable for any loss incurred while they are working for you.*

---

bond|ing /bɒndɪŋ/

COMMERCIAL INSURANCE

NOUN **Bonding** is a type of insurance that insures companies against theft, damage, or embezzlement carried out by its employees while they are working.

○ *Bonding is required to provide protection to the company against loss due to fraud, theft, forgery, or dishonesty.*

○ *In bonding, the surety agent always has the right to try to collect its losses from the person bonded, whereas in insurance the insurer may not attempt to recover losses from the insured.*

---

bo|nus /boʊnəs/ (bonuses)

LIFE INSURANCE

NOUN A **bonus** is a sum of money that an insurance company pays to its policyholders, for example a percentage of the company's profits.

○ *Several insurers have announced bonus cuts for holders of their life policies.*

○ *If the company does well for the year, a bonus may be paid out to the policyholders in the form of cash, or an increase in the amount of policy benefits.*

---

book of busi|ness /bʊk əv bɪznɪs/ (**books of business**)

COMMERCIAL INSURANCE

NOUN A company's or agent's **book of business** is the total of all insurance accounts written by them.

○ *The fundamental objective of underwriting is to produce a safe and profitable book of business.*

○ *In reinsurance, an insurer pays to place part of an insured risk or an entire book of business with one or more reinsurers.*

---

bor|de|reau /bɔrdərou/ (**bordereaus**)

REINSURANCE

NOUN A **bordereau** is a memorandum or invoice prepared for a company by an underwriter, containing a list of reinsured risks. It was originally a French term.

○ *Details of every risk ceded to the reinsurer are forwarded in the form of a bordereau.*

○ *A bordereau must be furnished periodically by the reinsured, giving details of reinsurance premiums or reinsurance losses.*

---

bro|ker|age /broukərɪdʒ/

SALES AND DISTRIBUTION

NOUN **Brokerage** is the money paid to an insurance broker.

○ *Brokerage fees paid to brokers are part of the expenses directly related to acquiring insurance or reinsurance accounts.*

○ *Brokerage costs are the premium commissions paid to insurance intermediaries for providing business.*

busi|ness in|ter|rup|tion in|sur|ance /bɪznɪs ɪntərʌpʃᵊn ɪnʃʊərəns/

COMMERCIAL INSURANCE

NOUN **Business interruption insurance** is insurance coverage that pays for loss of earnings when business operations have to stop because of property loss due to an insured danger.

○ *A policy that protects a company from loss of sales if a fire in a factory prevents it from carrying out its business functions is often referred to as business interruption insurance.*

○ *Weather insurance is a type of business interruption insurance that compensates for financial losses caused by adverse weather conditions, such as constant rain on the day scheduled for a major outdoor concert.*

▶ SYNONYM:
  business income insurance

COMMERCIAL INSURANCE

The following are further types of insurance that can be taken out by commercial organizations:

business overhead expense insurance, fire insurance, fleet insurance, forced place insurance, key man insurance, plate glass insurance, product liability insurance, professional liability insurance

---

busi|ness o|ver|head ex|pense in|sur|ance /bɪznɪs oʊvərhɛd ɪkspɛns ɪnʃʊərəns/

COMMERCIAL INSURANCE

NOUN **Business overhead expense insurance** is a disability policy which covers the business rather than the business owner for operating expenses when the business owner becomes totally disabled.

○ *Business overhead expense insurance is designed to pay necessary business overhead expenses, such as rent, should the insured business owner become disabled.*

○ *Business overhead expense insurance is disability insurance that steps in and pays the business expenses of a business owner while he is disabled.*

Cc

---

cal|cu|late a pre|mi|um /kælkyəleɪt ə priːmiəm/ (**calculates a premium, calculated a premium, calculating a premium**)

UNDERWRITING

PHRASE If you **calculate a premium**, you decide how much a policyholder has to pay for insurance cover.

○ *Premiums are calculated based on the applicant's risk level of incurring a loss.*

○ *Hazard forecasts are used for such things as calculating premiums and drawing up building codes.*

---

cal|cu|late a risk /kælkyəleɪt ə rɪsk/ (**calculates a risk, calculated a risk, calculating a risk**)

UNDERWRITING

PHRASE If you **calculate a risk**, you decide how likely an event is, whether the insurer should underwrite the risk, and at what cost.

○ *Insurance companies use mortality tables to help them calculate the risk that members of various age groups will die.*

○ *Actuaries use probability and statistics to calculate risk for insurance companies.*

---

can|cel a pol|i|cy /kæns²l ə pɒlisi/ (**cancels a policy, canceled a policy, canceling a policy**)

GENERAL

PHRASE If you **cancel a policy**, you terminate a contract of insurance.

○ *The insurance company cannot cancel the policy, provided that the policyholder continues to pay the premiums.*

○ *If you cancel this policy, you may be entitled to a full or partial refund of premium under the applicable rules and regulations.*

cap|tive /ˈkæptɪv/ (captives)

GENERAL

NOUN A **captive** is an insurance company set up by a commercial company to write the parent company's own insurances and obtain access to the reinsurance market.

○ Consumers who don't know that the agent is a captive, don't know that the advice on the best insurance is likely to be influenced by the fact that the owner of the firm is an insurance company.

○ Owning a captive is a means of arranging for self-insurance, with coverage for very large losses being arranged by the company by means of reinsurance.

cash plan /kæʃ plæn/ (cash plans)

MEDICAL INSURANCE

NOUN A **cash plan** is money paid towards the insured's optical or dental costs, and also admission to a hospital.

○ Another method of private health provision is a hospital cash plan to pay to the policyholder a fixed daily sum for time spent in the hospital.

○ A hospital cash plan is a low cost alternative to private medical insurance, providing fixed cash benefits for various circumstances.

cas|u|al|ty /ˈkæʒuəlti/ (casualties)

GENERAL

NOUN A **casualty** is a loss resulting from an accident, or someone who is hurt or killed in an accident.

○ Crime insurance is a form of casualty insurance that covers the policyholder against losses arising from the criminal acts of third parties.

○ The development of salvage-friendly vessels and crews can be a positive element in preventing a casualty or mitigating its effects in an emergency.

ca|tas|tro|phe ex|cess of loss /kəˈtæstrəfi ˈɛksɛs əv lɔs/

REINSURANCE

PHRASE **Catastrophe excess of loss** is a form of excess of loss reinsurance where the reinsurer agrees to reimburse the amount of a very large loss in excess of a particular sum.

○ Catastrophe excess of loss reinsurance protects the insurance company against an accumulation of losses due to single events such as major natural or human-made disasters.

○ *Catastrophe excess of loss reinsurance was developed after the San Francisco earthquake in 1906 to protect insurers against exceptional loss.*

---

cat|a|stroph|ic ill|ness /kætəstrɒfɪk ɪlnɪs/ (**catastrophic illnesses**)

MEDICAL INSURANCE

NOUN A **catastrophic illness** is a major health event that takes place during a particular period of time, such as a heart attack, stroke, or cancer.

○ *The high-deductible policy helped him lower his insurance premiums while preserving their coverage in case he or his wife suffered a catastrophic illness or injury.*

○ *The policy covers the initial, frequently routine, costs of healthcare, but may not cover all costs in the event of a catastrophic illness or serious injury.*

▶ **SYNONYM:**
critical illness

---

ce|dant /siːdᵊnt/ (**cedants**)

REINSURANCE

NOUN The **cedant** is the person or company that cedes business to another person or company.

○ *A reinsurer may agree to deposit a proportion of the reinsurance premium as a reserve for unearned premiums, which is then set aside by the cedant for future liabilities.*

○ *The cedant is paid a predetermined percentage of the profit realized by the reinsurer on the business ceded.*

> **WORD BUILDER**
> **-ant** = doing or causing something
>
> The suffix **-ant** often appears in words connected with doing something or causing something: **annuitant**, **cedant**, **claimant**, **tenant**.

---

cede /siːd/ (**cedes, ceded, ceding**)

REINSURANCE

VERB If a company or person **cedes** business, they reinsure their liability with another company or person, transferring the risk from an insurance company to a reinsurance company.

○ *Insurers can share a portion of their risks, up to 10 percent of their book of business, and each insurer chooses which risks to cede.*

○ *After the insurer keeps its share of the risk, the remainder is ceded to the reinsurer, so the reinsurer shares proportionately in the risk.*

▶ COLLOCATIONS:
cede a risk
cede business

---

churn /tʃɜrn/ (churns, churned, churning)

SALES AND DISTRIBUTION

VERB If a bank or broker **churns** a contract or policyholder, they encourage a client to change investments or policies in order to increase commissions at the client's expense.

○ *There was no evidence that contracts were fraudulent or had been deliberately churned by brokers in order to earn commission.*

○ *An agent should not engage in churning client policies, simply so that they can earn a new commission.*

---

civ|il un|rest /sɪvəl ʌnrɛst/

COMMERCIAL INSURANCE

NOUN **Civil unrest** is fighting between different groups of people living in the same country, and losses caused by this fighting are usually not covered by insurance.

○ *If the risk is assessed as being particularly severe, for example countries at war or with civil unrest, coverage may be refused.*

○ *Political risk insurance is advisable if you are traveling to countries where there is likely to be civil unrest.*

---

claim¹ /kleɪm/ (claims)

CLAIMS

NOUN A **claim** is a request to an insurance company for payment of a sum of money according to the terms of an insurance policy.

○ *Over the course of 30 or 40 years there may be only a handful of times you need to make an insurance claim.*

○ *Your employer is responsible for all issues related to your employment and your claim for workers' compensation.*

---

claim² /kleɪm/ (**claims**)

CLAIMS

NOUN A **claim** is a sum of money demanded from an insurance company according to the terms of an insurance policy.

○ *The employer assumes all or part of the responsibility for paying the health insurance claims of the employees.*

○ *A deductible is an amount deducted from an insurance claim.*

---

claim³ /kleɪm/ (**claims, claimed, claiming**)

CLAIMS

VERB If you **claim** money from an insurance company, you ask for payment of costs relating to a loss or damage for which you have insurance cover.

○ *If you claim for damage or loss to your insured property which occurs after your building has not been occupied for 60 consecutive days, an additional compulsory excess is payable.*

○ *The notice must specify the amount claimed or the facts that will enable the insurer to determine the amount.*

---

claim|ant /kleɪmənt/ (**claimants**)

CLAIMS

NOUN A **claimant** is a person requesting money from an insurer according to the terms of an insurance contract.

○ *An amount representing actual or potential liabilities is allocated by an insurer to cover obligations to policyholders and third-party claimants.*

○ *The insurer has to prove why they disagree with what the claimant claims he or she is entitled to.*

PEOPLE USING INSURANCE SERVICES

annuitant, beneficiary, claimant, retiree

claim form /kleɪm fɔrm/ (**claim forms**)

CLAIMS

NOUN A **claim form** is a standard printed document used for submitting a claim.

○ *Under normal circumstances, reimbursement will take place within ten days of receipt and approval of claim form and all required documents.*

○ *Your doctor will normally be asked to submit an attending physician's statement, along with a completed claim form.*

claims in|ves|ti|ga|tor /kleɪmz ɪnvɛstɪgeɪtər/ (**claims investigators**)

CLAIMS

NOUN A **claims investigator** is a person who is employed by an insurance company to obtain information necessary to evaluate a claim.

○ *Seeking information with respect to a pending claim is the normal responsibility of a claims investigator.*

○ *Insurance claims investigators play a key role in catching people who submit false information about fires.*

claims no|ti|fi|ca|tion /kleɪmz noʊtɪfɪkeɪʃªn/

CLAIMS

NOUN **Claims notification** is the process of informing an insurance company that a loss has occurred and that the policyholder intends to ask for money as a result.

○ *Losses are reported immediately, with generous reserves established within days or weeks of claims notification.*

○ *Some policies have high demands in relation to claims notification, requiring immediate notice or at best notification as soon as possible.*

claims ra|ti|o /kleɪmz reɪʃoʊ/ (**claims ratios**)

CLAIMS

NOUN The **claims ratio** is the percentage of claims costs incurred in relation to the premiums earned.

○ *There are two main reasons why this business is profitable: the premiums are not cheap, and the claims ratio is low.*

○ *The claims ratio is equal to the claims rate divided by the risk premium rate.*

RELATED WORDS

Compare this with the **combined ratio**, which is the combination of the insurer's loss ratio and expense ratio, and the **loss ratio**, which is the amount of money that an insurance company pays out in one year, divided by the amount of money that it receives in premiums.

CO|BRA /ˈkoʊbrə/ (short for **Consolidated Omnibus Budget Reconciliation Act**)

MEDICAL INSURANCE

ABBREVIATION In the U.S., **COBRA** insurance provides continuation of group health coverage insurance after an employee may have lost health insurance benefits at the end of employment.

○ *When you stop working for an employer, they will probably offer you COBRA medical coverage.*

○ *When coverage ends, you will be offered the option of extending coverage under COBRA.*

---

co|in|sur|ance /ˈkoʊɪnʃʊərəns/

REINSURANCE

NOUN **Coinsurance** is a method of insurance by which property is insured for a percentage of its value by a commercial insurance policy while the owner has liability for the remainder.

○ *A coinsurance is a percentage of the allowed amount that the patient must pay.*

○ *Coinsurance is a means whereby insurance companies enforce property limits to total value.*

WORD BUILDER
co- = with

The prefix **co-** often appears in words connected with doing something with another person or organization: **coinsurance**, **coinsure**, **coinsurer**, **copay**.

co|in|sure /koʊɪnʃʊər/ (coinsures, coinsured, coinsuring)

REINSURANCE

VERB If you **coinsure** property, you insure it jointly with another person or company.

○ *$6 million worth of real assets had been discovered, which was enough to pay back the four companies which had coinsured the fraudulent policies.*

○ *The insurance covers the policyholder, as well as coinsured persons, in the event that damage is suffered in connection with ownership or use of the yacht.*

co|in|sur|er /koʊɪnʃʊərər/ (coinsurers)

REINSURANCE

NOUN A **coinsurer** is a person or company whose policy covers the same risk as that of another person or company, and shares the loss.

○ *A coinsurer is any insurance provider offering joint coverage for a given property or entity in collaboration with another carrier.*

○ *If coverage is carried for only $40,000 then the insured is a coinsurer for $40,000 of the $80,000, and the insurance company would be responsible for the same amount.*

col|lide with /kəlaɪd wɪθ/ (collides with, collided with, colliding with)

VEHICLE INSURANCE

VERB If a vehicle **collides with** another vehicle or a person, it hits something or someone that is traveling in a different direction.

○ *If your automobile collides with a person's house, you are responsible for the cost of repairs and expenses associated with alternative living arrangements.*

○ *When your car sustains damage that did not result from colliding with another motor vehicle or object, the comprehensive portion of your policy will pay for the damages.*

col|li|sion cov|er|age /kəlɪʒᵊn kʌvərɪdʒ/

VEHICLE INSURANCE

NOUN **Collision coverage** is insurance cover for vehicle accidents.

○ *If you have collision coverage under your auto policy, you can choose to have your insurer pay your loss, minus your deductible.*

○ *Transportation coverage provides collision coverage for your mobile home and its contents against damage by collision or upset while being transported from one location to another.*

---

col|li|sion dam|age waiv|er /kəlɪʒᵊn dæmɪdʒ weɪvər/ (**collision damage waivers**)

VEHICLE INSURANCE

NOUN A **collision damage waiver** is a motor policy that covers accidental damage to an insured rental vehicle.

○ *Either you pay the car rental company $10 a day for a collision damage waiver, or you agree to pay the first $3,000 in damage caused to the car if it's damaged in a collision during your rental.*

○ *This contract offers, for an additional charge, a collision damage waiver to cover your financial responsibility for damage to the rental vehicle.*

---

com|bined ra|ti|o /kəmbaɪnd reɪʃoʊ/ (**combined ratios**)

CLAIMS

NOUN The **combined ratio** of an insurer or a reinsurer is the combination of its loss ratio and expense ratio.

○ *A combined ratio of less than 100 percent indicates underwriting profitability, while anything over 100 indicates an underwriting loss.*

○ *A decrease in the combined ratio means financial results are improving; an increase means they are deteriorating.*

---

com|mis|sion /kəmɪʃᵊn/

SALES AND DISTRIBUTION

NOUN If an insurance company pays **commission** to an intermediary, they pay them a fee for selling an insurance policy.

○ *Insurance agents are paid a commission on a homeowner's insurance policy which is a percentage of the premium.*

○ *An agent may be employed by a particular insurance company to sell insurance policies on its behalf and handle claims, receiving a commission on sales.*

---

com|mu|ta|tion /kɒmyəteɪʃᵊn/

LIFE INSURANCE: PENSIONS

NOUN **Commutation** is the formal ending of an insurance or reinsurance agreement by payment of an agreed sum in settlement.

○ *The commutation clause provides, by payment of a lump sum, for the complete discharge of all future obligations for reinsurance losses incurred.*

○ *Commutation involves the termination of all obligations between the parties to a reinsurance agreement, normally accompanied by a final cash settlement.*

---

com|mute /kəmyu̱t/ (commutes, commuted, commuting)

LIFE INSURANCE: PENSIONS

VERB If you **commute** an annuity, you pay it at one time instead of in installments.

○ *Retirement annuities are taxed as earned income, but part of the benefits can be commuted to a tax free lump sum.*

○ *If you leave the plan before age 55, you may take a deferred pension or transfer the commuted value of your pension to another retirement arrangement.*

---

com|pre|hen|sive /kɒmprɪhe̱nsɪv/

VEHICLE INSURANCE

ADJECTIVE A **comprehensive** motor insurance policy provides protection against most risks, including third-party liability, fire, theft, and damage.

○ *Comprehensive coverage protects against damage to your automobile from acts of nature or other events not associated with operating the automobile.*

○ *The comprehensive policy covers damage to the policyholder's car not resulting from a collision with another car and theft.*

▶ **COLLOCATIONS:**
comprehensive coverage
comprehensive insurance
comprehensive policy

---

con|do|min|i|um (INFORMAL condo) /kɒndəmɪ̱niəm/ (condominiums)

RESIDENCE INSURANCE

NOUN A **condominium** is an apartment in a building with several apartments, each of which is owned by the people living in it.

○ *A condominium property requires special insurance treatment, as each apartment is a unit and the stairways, pathways, and parking areas are in common ownership.*

C

○ With condominium insurance, the interior of your unit, your personal possessions, or personal liability are not covered by your association's insurance.

---

con|do own|er /kɒndoʊ oʊnər/ (**condo owners**)

RESIDENCE INSURANCE

NOUN A **condo owner** is the owner of a condominium.

○ A separate policy paid for in part by each condo owner's monthly maintenance fee covers all the common areas of the building as well as the building systems themselves.

○ The property act provides that a condominium association may require condo owners to obtain insurance coverage.

---

con|se|quen|tial loss /kɒnsɪkwɛnʃəl lɒs/ (**consequential losses**)

CLAIMS

NOUN A **consequential loss** is a loss that follows another loss that is caused by a danger that has been insured against.

○ The loss of ongoing profit because of the inability to continue trading is a consequential loss.

○ If a cold storage plant is without electrical power, and foodstuffs spoil as a result, then this is a consequential loss, not a direct loss.

---

con|tin|gen|cy /kəntɪndʒənsi/ (**contingencies**)

GENERAL

NOUN A **contingency** is an event or situation that might happen in the future, especially one that could cause problems.

○ Insurers base their premium rates and their willingness to accept risks partly on the probability that certain contingencies will or will not occur.

○ The insurer agrees to pay on behalf of the policyholder for covered losses, up to the limits purchased, caused by the designated contingencies listed in the policy.

---

con|tri|bu|tion[1] /kɒntrɪbyuʃən/ (**contributions**)

REINSURANCE

NOUN A **contribution** is a portion of the total liability of each of two or more companies for a risk for which all of them have issued policies.

○ *Under the contribution by equal shares method, each policy is required to contribute the same amount until the limit of one policy is exhausted.*

○ *Each company's contribution will ensure that they share equally in the loss until the share of each insurer equals the lowest limit of liability under any policy or until the full amount of loss is paid.*

con|tri|bu|tion² /kɒntrɪbyuʃən/ (**contributions**)

`LIFE INSURANCE: PENSIONS`

NOUN A **contribution** is a payment into a retirement savings or pension plan.

○ *Factors such as a client's age, income, length of time before retirement, and rate of return of the investment portfolio impact the required annual contribution amount.*

○ *The contribution into your retirement fund made by your employer up to 12.5 percent of your basic salary is exempt from tax.*

con|trib|u|to|ry /kəntrɪbyətɔri/

`LIFE INSURANCE`

ADJECTIVE A **contributory** insurance or pension scheme is one in which the premiums are paid partly by the employer and partly by the employees who benefit from it.

○ *A contributory fund is a fund to which members make contributions, deducted from weekly wages or monthly salaries.*

○ *With a contributory plan, the employees pay part of the premiums of a group life, health, or pension policy.*

> **RELATED WORDS**
>
> The opposite of this is **noncontributory**, where the total cost of premiums are paid by the company.

con|vert|i|ble term in|sur|ance /kənvɜrtɪbəl tɜrm ɪnʃʊərəns/

`LIFE INSURANCE`

NOUN A **convertible term insurance** is a life insurance policy which pays out if the policyholder dies within a specified period of time, but also allows them to convert to another type of plan.

○ *Once the term of a convertible term insurance has expired, the policyholder has the choice to convert the plan to a different type of contract which can be a further term plan, an endowment, or a whole of life contract.*

○ *A convertible term insurance can be converted to a permanent or whole life policy without evidence of insurability, subject to time limitations.*

---

cool|ing-off pe|ri|od /kulɪŋ ɔf pɪəriəd/ (**cooling-off periods**)

SALES AND DISTRIBUTION

NOUN A **cooling-off period** is a set time limit within which policyholders have the right to cancel an insurance policy without any penalty.

○ *The consumer must be given the opportunity to withdraw from the concluded contract without incurring liability during the cooling-off period.*

○ *There will be a cooling-off period of fourteen days following the issuance of a new policy to allow a purchaser to cancel the agreement.*

---

co|pay /koʊpeɪ/

MEDICAL INSURANCE

NOUN **Copay** is the amount of a medical service or prescription that a patient is responsible for, while the insurance company covers the remaining cost.

○ *For routine doctor visits, there's usually a copay, or a small flat fee.*

○ *If you have additional doctor's visits or hospitalizations, once you've met your deductible, you will only pay the designated copay amount.*

---

cov|er¹ /kʌvər/ (**covers, covered, covering**)

GENERAL

VERB If an insurance policy **covers** a person or a particular risk, it insures them against loss or risk.

○ *Water damage from floods is covered under separate flood insurance policies.*

○ *An underinsured policyholder may only receive part of the cost of replacing or repairing damaged items covered in the policy.*

---

cov|er² /kʌvər/

GENERAL

NOUN **Cover** is the extent of the protection provided by insurance.

○ When choosing cover for overseas travel, make sure the policy will be recognized around the world.

○ The length of cover can be extended even if the amount paid is not being increased.

▶ SYNONYM:
coverage

cov|er|age /kʌvərɪdʒ/

GENERAL

NOUN **Coverage** is the extent of the protection provided by insurance.

○ Flood coverage is excluded under homeowners' policies and many commercial property policies.

○ Personal property used in a business has been added to the policy under this extension of coverage.

▶ SYNONYM:
cover

C|P|I /siː piː aɪ/ (short for **Consumer Price Index**)

LIFE INSURANCE: PENSIONS

ABBREVIATION The **CPI** is an official measure of the rate of inflation within a country's economy.

○ The adjustment can raise or lower the annuity benefit for the next year, depending on changes in CPI.

○ An indexed life insurance policy is usually tied to the CPI so that death benefits increase according to the rate of inflation.

crash¹ /kræʃ/ (crashes, crashed, crashing)

VEHICLE INSURANCE

VERB If a moving vehicle **crashes**, it hits something and is damaged or destroyed.

○ Because it pays regardless of fault, the insurance would cover your medical expenses if you were to crash your car into a fence post.

○ Automobile insurance includes an aspect of liability insurance that indemnifies against the harm that a crashing car can cause to others' lives, health, or property.

C

crash² /kræʃ/ (crashes)

VEHICLE INSURANCE

NOUN A **crash** is an accident in which a moving vehicle hits something else and is damaged or destroyed.

○ This coverage pays for damages you or members of your family cause to other people's property in a crash involving a motor vehicle.

○ After he was injured in the car crash, he was contacted by two insurance companies – his own, and the carrier for the car that hit him.

cred|it card in|sur|ance /krɛdɪt kɑrd ɪnʃʊərəns/

COMMERCIAL INSURANCE

NOUN **Credit card insurance** is coverage for situations in which someone fraudulently uses your credit card.

○ Credit card insurance covers you for losses incurred if your credit card is lost or stolen.

○ Credit card insurance is advisable, especially as the fraudulent use of lost or stolen credit and debit cards is on the increase.

crit|i|cal ill|ness in|sur|ance /krɪtɪkəl ɪlnɪs ɪnʃʊərəns/

MEDICAL INSURANCE

NOUN **Critical illness insurance** is an insurance policy which pays out if the policyholder is diagnosed with a serious medical condition, such as a stroke, cancer, or heart disease.

○ Some forms of critical illness insurance also offer policyholders suffering, for example, from cancer the option to travel to highly specialized hospitals in other countries to receive treatment.

○ A lump sum critical illness insurance policy will pay a designated amount of money to you when you are diagnosed with a covered critical illness such as cancer, stroke, or heart attack.

Dd

dam|age¹ /dæmɪdʒ/ (**damages, damaged, damaging**)

General

VERB If you **damage** something or part of someone's body, you cause physical harm.

- ○ Public liability insurance covers a business against claims should its operations injure a member of the public or damage their property in some way.

- ○ If the operator of the boat accidentally damages another boat or injures some swimmers, there would be protection.

dam|age² /dæmɪdʒ/

General

NOUN **Damage** is physical harm that is done to something or to a part of someone's body.

- ○ Coverage for flood and earthquake damage is excluded and must be purchased separately.

- ○ Liability insurance covers what the policyholder is legally obligated to pay because of bodily injury or property damage caused to another person.

D|&|O in|sur|ance /diː ənd oʊ ɪnʃʊərəns/ (short for **Directors and Officers insurance**)

General

ABBREVIATION **D&O insurance** is a personal liability insurance that provides cover to the directors and senior executives of a company.

- ○ D&O insurance covers company directors and officers in the event that they are accused of wrongdoing while conducting company business.

- ○ Serving as a director is made more dangerous by the prospect that a bankruptcy court may limit or bar coverage otherwise provided under a D&O insurance policy.

RELATED WORDS

Compare to **key man insurance**, which is an insurance policy taken out by a small company on the life of a senior executive whose death would create a serious loss.

---

death ben|e|fits /dɛθ bɛnɪfɪts/

[LIFE INSURANCE]

NOUN **Death benefits** are the amount of money that an insurance policy will pay upon the death of the person whose life is being insured.

○ *This type of combined life insurance offers accelerated death benefits to those diagnosed with a terminal illness and expected to die within 12 months.*

○ *The payments made while the insured is living are deducted from any death benefits paid to beneficiaries.*

---

de|ceased /dɪsi̱st/ (**deceased**)

[LIFE INSURANCE]

NOUN **The deceased** is the person who has died.

○ *The executor is the person named in a will to manage the estate of the deceased according to the terms of the will.*

○ *If the worker died before becoming eligible for retirement benefits, the survivor would have to wait to receive 75 percent of the combined benefit until the deceased would have become eligible.*

---

de|creas|ing term in|sur|ance /dɪkri̱sɪŋ tɜrm ɪnʃʊərəns/

[LIFE INSURANCE]

NOUN **Decreasing term insurance** is life insurance with the amount of coverage decreasing over the term of the policy and a lump sum payment if you die in advance.

○ *Coverage is in decreasing term insurance, so the amount of coverage decreases as the debt decreases.*

○ *A big portion of the decreasing term insurance found today is in the form of mortgage life insurance, which pegs its benefit to the remaining mortgage on the insured's home.*

de|duct|i|ble¹ /dɪdʌktɪbəl/

COMMERCIAL INSURANCE

ADJECTIVE A **deductible** amount is an amount deducted from payment due from an insurance premium, that must be paid by the insured person.

○ *The policy pays only for the amount of loss which exceeds the deductible amount shown in the Declarations.*

○ *When the amount of health care expense exceeds the deductible amount, the insurance company will pay for it.*

de|duct|i|ble² /dɪdʌktɪbəl/ (**deductibles**)

COMMERCIAL INSURANCE

NOUN A **deductible** is a sum of money that you have to pay toward the cost of an insurance claim when the insurance company pays the rest.

○ *Her auto insurance policy has a $500 deductible on collision coverage.*

○ *The insured is responsible for the deductible, which is the first $500 of damage, and the insurance company pays the balance.*

de|ferred an|nu|i|ty /dɪfɜrd ənuɪti/ (**deferred annuities**)

LIFE INSURANCE

NOUN A **deferred annuity** is an annuity that begins not less than one year after the final purchase premium.

○ *When you are ready to receive income payments, the deferred annuity provides many choices, including guaranteed income for life.*

○ *With an immediate annuity, payments commence right away, in contrast to a deferred annuity, under which the payments do not commence until later.*

de|ferred pe|ri|od (also known as **waiting period** or **excess period**) /dɪfɜrd pɪəriəd/ (**deferred periods**)

MEDICAL INSURANCE

NOUN The **deferred period** is the period of time from when a person has become unable to work until the time that the benefit begins to be paid.

○ *He selected a deferred period of six months because he knew he would receive sick pay from his company for that period and wouldn't need the insurance benefits.*

> ○ *Benefits are payable when the policyholder becomes incapacitated and after the deferred period has passed.*

---

de|fined ben|e|fit plan /dɪfaɪnd bɛnɪfɪt plæn/ (defined benefit plans)

| LIFE INSURANCE: PENSIONS |

NOUN A **defined benefit plan** is a type of pension plan that guarantees a lifetime income upon retirement based on the employee's income and years of service.

> ○ *A defined benefit plan is a qualified retirement plan in which annual contributions are made to fund a chosen level of retirement income at a predetermined future retirement date.*

> ○ *A defined benefit plan pays participants a specific retirement benefit that is promised in the plan document.*

---

de|fined con|tri|bu|tion plan /dɪfaɪnd kɒntrɪbyuʃ°n plæn/ (defined contribution plans)

| LIFE INSURANCE: PENSIONS |

NOUN A **defined contribution plan** is a type of pension plan that specifies the annual contribution that the employer will pay on behalf of each plan participant.

> ○ *In a defined contribution plan, the sponsor or company makes contributions to an investment fund in the plan member's account.*

> ○ *A defined contribution plan is a tax-qualified retirement plan in which an employer's annual contributions are determined by a formula set for those in the plan.*

---

de|fraud /dɪfrɔd/ (defrauds, defrauded, defrauding)

| GENERAL |

VERB If someone **defrauds** an insurer, they deliberately deceive them in order to gain insurance benefits.

> ○ *Providing inaccurate information with the intent to receive a lower premium is considered intent to defraud.*

> ○ *He was accused of obtaining the policy by presenting false information and concealing information that was material to the policy, with the intent to defraud the issuer of the policy.*

den|tal care /dɛntəl kɛər/

MEDICAL INSURANCE

NOUN **Dental care** is medical care and hygiene relating to your teeth.

○ This coverage will help pay for dental treatment and allow you to make decisions about your dental care based on need rather than cost.

○ Some healthcare plans include dental care, while others have a policy clause excluding the care and treatment of teeth and gums.

den|tal in|sur|ance /dɛntəl ɪnʃʊərəns/

MEDICAL INSURANCE

NOUN **Dental insurance** is insurance that pays for treatment by a dentist.

○ Dental insurance covers the cost of routine dental care along with accidental damage to your teeth.

○ Dental insurance includes benefits for oral examinations and X-rays as well as preventive dental treatment.

de|ny a claim /dɪnaɪ ə kleɪm/ (**denies a claim, denied a claim, denying a claim**)

CLAIMS

PHRASE If an insurance company **denies a claim**, it refuses to pay a claim submitted by a policyholder.

○ Exclusions are specific events or circumstances where the insurance company has the right to deny a claim.

○ Punitive damages may only be assessed against an insurer when the insurer denies a claim without an arguable or legitimate basis.

de|pend|ent /dɪpɛndənt/ (**dependents**)

LIFE INSURANCE

NOUN A **dependent** is a person, especially a child or spouse, who depends on you for food, clothes, and money.

○ If a federal employee dies from a work-related injury, a cash compensation is paid to the worker's surviving dependents.

○ The policy covers the employees and their spouses and dependents for 18 months after their employment is terminated.

de|pre|ci|ate /dɪpriːʃieɪt/ (depreciates, depreciated, depreciating)

RESIDENCE INSURANCE

VERB If an insured item **depreciates**, it decreases in value.

○ The policy covers the cost to replace a personal item even though you might have owned it for a number of years and it has depreciated in value.

○ The property was valued at $100,000 new, but has depreciated in value by 20 percent since the insurance policy was taken out.

> **WORD FAMILY**
>
> **depreciate VERB** ○ The equipment will depreciate fairly rapidly.
>
> **depreciation NOUN** ○ Because of depreciation, the vehicles are now worth much less than their purchase price.
>
> The adjective **depreciable** is used for items whose loss of value can be set against tax.

de|pre|ci|a|tion /dɪpriːʃieɪʃᵊn/

RESIDENCE INSURANCE

NOUN **Depreciation** is the reduction in the value or price of an insured item.

○ Replacement cost coverage pays the cost of replacing your property regardless of depreciation or appreciation.

○ Under recovery on the basis of full replacement cost, the owner suffers no reduction in loss recovery due to depreciation of the property from its original value.

di|rect in|sur|er /dɪrɛkt ɪnʃʊərər/ (direct insurers)

SALES AND DISTRIBUTION

NOUN A **direct insurer** is an insurance company that sells its policies directly to customers without using intermediaries.

○ Direct insurers can charge lower premiums because they don't need to pay commission to intermediaries.

○ A reinsurer insures derivative risks, which are the risks assumed by a direct insurer.

dis|a|bil|i|ty clause /dɪsəbɪlɪti klɔz/ (disability clauses)

MEDICAL INSURANCE

NOUN A **disability clause** is a clause in life insurance policies enabling you to stop paying premiums without loss of coverage and often to receive a pension if you become permanently disabled.

○ *The disability clause provides that certain benefits will be paid in the event the insured becomes totally and permanently disabled from an accident or sickness.*

○ *The disability clause entitles a policyholder who becomes permanently disabled to stop premium payments without loss of life insurance.*

dis|a|bil|i|ty in|sur|ance /dɪsəbɪlɪti ɪnʃʊərəns/

MEDICAL INSURANCE

NOUN **Disability insurance** is insurance that pays disability benefit as a partial replacement of income lost due to illness or injury.

○ *Social Security provides disability insurance for workers who lose their capacity to work before they reach retirement age.*

○ *Long-term disability insurance provides coverage in the form of monthly income payments for as long as the insured remains disabled.*

dis|a|bled /dɪseɪbəld/

MEDICAL INSURANCE

ADJECTIVE If a person is **disabled**, they are unable to use one or more parts of their body properly.

○ *A medical examination may also be used to determine whether an insured claiming disability is actually disabled.*

○ *If you become totally disabled before age 60, your disability payments will continue until your disability ceases or until you reach age 65, whichever is first.*

dis|close /dɪsklouz/ (discloses, disclosed, disclosing)

UNDERWRITING

VERB If you **disclose** information to an insurer, you provide information about a risk that may be relevant when calculating the premium.

○ *Please fully disclose all material facts that are relevant to the policy including any disease or claims made by you.*

○ *If you disclose motoring convictions to an automobile insurer you will often have to pay an extra premium.*

---

dis|clo|sure /dɪsklouʒər/

UNDERWRITING

NOUN **Disclosure** is the provision of information about a risk to an insurer that may be relevant when calculating the premium.

○ *The strict requirement for full and honest disclosure is a fundamental principle of insurance.*

○ *Before entering into a life or income protection contract, a person has a duty of disclosure to reveal anything that they know which could affect the decision of the insurance company to accept the risk.*

---

dis|or|der /dɪsɔrdər/

MEDICAL INSURANCE

NOUN A **disorder** is a mental or physical illness which prevents part of your body from working properly.

○ *Depending on the medical condition, the insurer may shorten the benefit period to compensate for the medical disorder.*

○ *Sleep disorders have been linked to an increased risk of injury due to falls and car accidents.*

> **WORD BUILDER**
> **dis-** = not
>
> The prefix **dis-** is often added to the beginning of words to form their opposite: **disability**, **disabled**, **disorder**.

---

dis|tri|bu|tion chan|nel /dɪstrɪbyuʃ°n tʃæn°l/ (distribution channels)

SALES AND DISTRIBUTION

NOUN A **distribution channel** is a method used by insurers to sell their products to customers.

○ *Exclusive agents, who are tied to a particular insurance company, are the most favored distribution channel from insurance companies' point of view.*

○ *Banks and post offices are the predominant life insurance distribution channel, accounting for 59 percent of sales in 2010.*

div|i|dend /dɪvɪdɛnd/ (**dividends**)

LIFE INSURANCE

NOUN A **dividend** is a sum of money from a company's net profits that is distributed to the holders of certain insurance policies.

○ *A mutual insurance company is owned by its policyholders, and returns part of its profits to the policyholders as dividends.*

○ *Dividends are cash payments credited to whole life policies generally as a percentage of current cash value.*

TALKING ABOUT DIVIDENDS

When a company **declares** a dividend, they say what the dividend will be. An **interim** dividend is paid before the end of a period, when a **final** dividend is paid or **issued**.

If you use a dividend to invest in something else, you **reinvest** it.

---

dou|ble in|dem|ni|ty /dʌbᵊl ɪndɛmnɪti/

LIFE INSURANCE

NOUN **Double indemnity** is a clause in life insurance policies that provides for the payment of double the policy's face value in the event of the policyholder's accidental death.

○ *Under the double indemnity rider, if death occurs through accident, the insurance payable is double the face amount.*

○ *Double indemnity pays twice the amount of the policy face value if death results from accidental causes, as if both a full coverage policy and an accidental death policy were in effect on the insured.*

---

draw a pen|sion /drɔ ə pɛnʃᵊn/ (**draws a pension, drew a pension, drawn a pension, drawing a pension**)

LIFE INSURANCE: PENSIONS

PHRASE If you **draw a pension**, you receive money from an insurer or the state because you have reached a particular age.

○ *Pensioners are required to authorize the branch from which they are drawing their pension to deduct the insurance premium.*

○ *The total amount of capital that you have saved for retirement should then be invested to earn interest to enable you to draw a pension.*

dy|nam|ic in|sur|ance /daɪnæmɪk ɪnʃʊərəns/

LIFE INSURANCE

NOUN **Dynamic insurance** is a type of insurance coverage where the policyholder can choose to increase benefits and premiums by a fixed percentage each year to offset the effects of inflation.

○ *Dynamic insurance is a suitable option for you if you want to protect your policy against inflation.*

○ *Because you have selected dynamic insurance, your premiums will increase by 2 percent every year.*

Ee

E|&|O /i ənd <u>ou</u>/ (short for **errors and omissions**)

UNDERWRITING

ABBREVIATION **E&O** is a professional liability insurance that protects companies and individuals against claims made by customers for inadequate work or negligence.

○ *E&O coverage protects the insured against liability for committing an error or omission in the performance of professional duties.*

○ *E&O covers the policyholder for negligent acts and omissions that may harm his or her clients.*

---

ear|ly re|tire|ment /ɜrli rɪta<u>ɪə</u>rmənt/

LIFE INSURANCE

NOUN **Early retirement** is a situation in which a person stops working earlier than at the usual statutory retirement age.

○ *When early retirement isn't planned, this places additional stress on the retirement plan because the individual has fewer assets that have to last a longer amount of time.*

○ *Any losses in pension resulting from early retirement are usually offset with attractive incentive payments.*

---

earth|quake /ɜrθkweɪk/ (**earthquakes**)

RESIDENCE INSURANCE

NOUN An **earthquake** is a sudden shaking of the earth's surface that often causes a lot of damage.

○ *The policy includes coverage for damage by shock and by fire occasioned by or happening through an earthquake.*

○ *Most of the devastation caused by earthquakes is a direct result of the ground shaking violently.*

earth|quake cov|er|age /ɜrθkweɪk kʌvərɪdʒ/

RESIDENCE INSURANCE

NOUN **Earthquake coverage** is insurance coverage for damage caused by earthquakes.

○ *Flood insurance, like earthquake coverage, is usually only of interest to those residents whose property is exposed.*

○ *If your business premises are shut down due to earthquake damage, you'll need to have earthquake coverage to be able to make a claim.*

E

el|i|gi|bil|i|ty /ɛlɪdʒɪbɪlɪti/

MEDICAL INSURANCE

NOUN **Eligibility** is the state of being eligible for something.

○ *Activities of daily living are used to measure the degree of impairment, and can affect eligibility for certain types of insurance benefits.*

○ *For some plans your country of citizenship determines eligibility for coverage in a certain country.*

el|i|gi|ble /ɛlɪdʒɪbəl/

MEDICAL INSURANCE

ADJECTIVE Someone who is **eligible for** something or **to do** something is qualified or allowed to do it.

○ *To be eligible for survivor annuity benefits, a child must have been dependent on the employee at the time of the employee's death.*

○ *You must be at least 55 with 10 years continuous employment to be eligible for full post-retirement benefits.*

▶ COLLOCATION:
  eligible for

e|mer|gen|cy room (ABBR **ER**, BRIT **A & E (accident and emergency))** /ɪmɜrdʒənsi rum/ (**emergency rooms**)

MEDICAL INSURANCE

NOUN The **emergency room** is the part of a hospital where people who have severe injuries or sudden illnesses are taken for emergency treatment.

○ *Some insurance plans won't cover a trip to the emergency room if the symptoms appeared more than 24 hours earlier.*

○ *If a person without health insurance is struck by a car they should not be left to die as soon as we determine that they can't pay for emergency room care.*

---

em|ploy|er-pro|vid|ed /ɪmplɔɪər prəvaɪdɪd/

`MEDICAL INSURANCE`

ADJECTIVE **Employer-provided** insurance is arranged or funded by the organization for which the policyholder works.

○ *The dominance of the insurance market by employer-provided plans means that the market for individual and small-group policies is underdeveloped and that the cost of such coverage is very high.*

○ *This plan helps reduce your company's costs by allowing employees to pay their portion of employer-provided health benefits with pre-tax dollars.*

---

en|dorse /ɪndɔrs/ (endorses, endorsed, endorsing)

`UNDERWRITING`

VERB If you **endorse** an insurance policy, you add a clause or amendment to it allowing for change of coverage.

○ *If you purchase crime insurance, the crime coverage can be endorsed to include the pension plan at no extra charge.*

○ *A written or oral contract, known as a binder, will be issued temporarily to place insurance in force when it is not possible to issue a new policy or endorse the existing policy immediately.*

---

en|dorse|ment /ɪndɔrsmənt/ (endorsements)

`UNDERWRITING`

NOUN An **endorsement** is a clause in or amendment to an insurance policy allowing for change of coverage.

○ *Many options and endorsements are available to tailor the plan to the policyholder's needs.*

○ *An endorsement can be added to an automobile policy that gives protection while the insured is driving a car other than the one named in the policy.*

en|dow|ment in|sur|ance /ɪndaʊmənt ɪnʃʊərəns/

LIFE INSURANCE

NOUN **Endowment insurance** is a type of life insurance that pays a particular sum directly to the policyholder at a stated date, or to a beneficiary if the policyholder dies before this date.

○ *Endowment insurance can be considered a type of savings plan, as it provides for a lump sum payment in the event the insured survives to the end of the specified period.*

○ *Endowment insurance is a type of life insurance contract designed to pay a lump sum after a specified term.*

en|dow|ment mort|gage /ɪndaʊmənt mɔrgɪdz/
(endowment mortgages)

LIFE INSURANCE

NOUN An **endowment mortgage** is a mortgage in which repayments are paid into a life insurance policy, and the loan is repaid by the policy either when it matures or when the policyholder dies.

○ *With an endowment mortgage, the insurance company issues the endowment policy, but often it is a bank or building society which supplies the mortgage.*

○ *In the UK, one of the most popular bancassurance products is the endowment mortgage, which is an endowment life insurance policy linked to a traditional mortgage.*

en|dow|ment pol|i|cy /ɪndaʊmənt pɒlɪsi/ **(endowment policies)**

LIFE INSURANCE

NOUN An **endowment policy** is an insurance policy that provides life coverage, but that pays a sum of money if the policyholder is still alive after an agreed period of time.

○ *An endowment policy is designed to provide a lump sum on maturity.*

○ *An endowment policy will pay you a fixed amount on a set date or if you die before that date; in other words it's both a way of saving and a life insurance policy.*

eq|ui|ty-linked pol|i|cy /ɛkwɪti lɪŋkt pɒlɪsi/ (**equity-linked policies**)

LIFE INSURANCE

NOUN An **equity-linked policy** is an insurance policy in which part or all of the premiums are invested in ordinary shares for the benefit of the beneficiaries of the policy.

○ *The payoff of an equity-linked policy depends on the performance of the shares invested in.*

○ *Unlike traditional life insurance policies, which provide a fixed benefit, the equity-linked policy transfers the full investment risk to the policyholder.*

es|ca|la|tion /ɛskəleɪʃ°n/

LIFE INSURANCE

NOUN **Escalation** is an increase in premiums or policy benefits in line with agreed factors, such as inflation.

○ *The extension does not provide automatic coverage for project over-run on account of price variation, as the maximum escalation permitted under the policy is 50 percent of the prime cost.*

○ *Escalation provides for automatic increases on a defined basis in premiums and sums insured.*

es|tate /ɪsteɪt/

LIFE INSURANCE

NOUN A person's **estate** is their property and money, especially everything that is left after they die.

○ *A personal representative is appointed through the will of a deceased or by a court to settle the estate of someone who dies.*

○ *A certified legal document, known as probate, must be in place to prove that a will is valid, thus allowing an executor to administer the estate of the deceased.*

es|ti|mat|ed max|i|mum loss /ɛstɪmeɪtɪd mæksɪməm lɒs/ (**estimated maximum losses**)

COMMERCIAL INSURANCE

NOUN **Estimated maximum loss** is the amount of risk that an underwriter estimates the insurer will be able to cover before ceding any surplus to a reinsurer.

○ *Possible maximum loss may arise from more remote scenarios than those for probable or estimated maximum loss, and therefore carry higher values.*

○ *Estimated maximum loss is a measure of exposure used in rating or to judge outwards reinsurance requirements.*

---

ex|cess /ɛksɛs/ (excesses)

COMMERCIAL INSURANCE

NOUN **Excess** is a stated contribution towards the cost of a claim that the policyholder has to pay.

○ *The excess is the lump sum that you pay in the event of an accident.*

○ *As a bigger excess reduces the financial risk carried by your insurer, your insurer is able to offer you a significantly lower premium.*

---

ex|cess of loss re|in|sur|ance /ɛksɛs əv lɒs riːɪnʃʊərəns/

REINSURANCE

NOUN **Excess of loss reinsurance** is a type of reinsurance whereby an insurer pays the amount of the loss for a particular risk up to an agreed limit.

○ *As is true with any form of excess of loss reinsurance, the reinsurance agreement includes a loss retention for the reinsured and a limit of reinsurance for the reinsurer.*

○ *Excess of loss reinsurance indemnifies the ceding company against loss in excess of specific retention.*

---

ex|clude a risk /ɪkskluːd ə rɪsk/ (excludes a risk, excluded a risk, excluding a risk)

UNDERWRITING

PHRASE If an insurance company **excludes a risk**, they declare that a particular risk is not covered by an insurance policy.

○ *Most property insurance policies exclude risks such as malfunction of a boiler or other machinery.*

○ *Almost all policies will exclude risks such as preexisting medical conditions from coverage, while others may exclude high-risk leisure activities.*

ex|clu|sion /ɪkskluːʒ³n/ (exclusions)

UNDERWRITING

NOUN An **exclusion** is a clause in an insurance policy that excludes particular losses or risks.

○ The coverage is not suitable for all circumstances due to the exclusions within the policy.

○ Exclusions common to the boat owner's package policy are portable electronic photographic or water sports equipment, or fishing gear.

ex|pe|ri|ence rat|ing /ɪkspɪəriəns reɪtɪŋ/

UNDERWRITING

NOUN **Experience rating** is a method of adjusting the premium for a risk based on past loss experience for that risk compared to loss experience for an average risk.

○ With experience rating, the insurer evaluates the claims history of a particular group in order to set a premium for the next period.

○ The company uses experience rating to review the previous year's claims experience for a group insurance contract in order to establish premiums for the future contract.

ex|pe|ri|ence ta|ble /ɪkspɪəriəns teɪb³l/ (experience tables)

LIFE INSURANCE

NOUN An **experience table** is a table, especially a morbidity table, that is based on past statistics.

○ The experience table of mortality states expected mortality rates based upon data accumulated from a large number of insured persons.

○ The experience table will give you the mortality rate expected at different ages.

ex|pi|ra|tion date /ɛkspɪreɪʃ³n deɪt/ (expiration dates)

GENERAL

NOUN The **expiration date** of an insurance policy is the date beyond which it is no longer valid and must be renewed.

○ Cancellation is the discontinuance of an insurance policy before its normal expiration date, either by the insured or the company.

○ The policy is in force from the beginning or effective date to the expiration date.

ex|pire /ɪkspaɪər/ (expires, expired, expiring)

GENERAL

VERB If an insurance policy **expires**, it is no longer valid.

○ At the end of the mortgage period the decreasing term insurance expires, leaving the base policy still in force.

○ A renewal policy will be issued to replace an expiring policy.

ex|posed to /ɪkspouzd tu/

UNDERWRITING

ADJECTIVE If you are **exposed to** a particular risk or hazard, you are in danger from it.

○ Occupational risks are risks that a life assured would be exposed to in performing the normal duties of their occupation.

○ A firefighter is exposed to much greater danger than an insurance clerk.

ex|po|sure /ɪkspouʒər/

UNDERWRITING

NOUN A company's **exposure** is the amount of a particular risk that it has.

○ Risk management involves analyzing all exposures to the possibility of loss to which a company might be subject, and determining how to handle these.

○ It may be better to pass some risk to a reinsurance company as this will reduce the insurer's exposure to risk.

Ff

fac|ul|ta|tive /fækəlteɪtɪv/

REINSURANCE

ADJECTIVE Facultative reinsurance is negotiated for each reinsurance, as the reinsurer has no obligation to accept a particular risk nor the insurer to reinsure.

○ Facultative contracts are negotiated separately for each insurance contract reinsured.

○ Facultative coverage is a form of reinsurance where the reinsurer accepts or rejects individual risks.

fend|er-bend|er /fɛndər bɛndər/ (**fender-benders**)

VEHICLE INSURANCE

NOUN A **fender-bender** is an informal term for a car accident in which little damage is done.

○ It is recommended that you purchase this coverage because if you are involved in a fender-bender with an uninsured motorist, it is highly unlikely you will receive any payment for damages if the other driver is at fault.

○ There are thousands of instances of fender-benders where these seemingly insignificant accidents have escalated into major disputes over liability.

file a claim /faɪl ə kleɪm/ (**files a claim, filed a claim, filing a claim**)

CLAIMS

PHRASE If you **file a claim**, you make a request to an insurance company for payment of a sum of money according to the terms of an insurance policy.

○ The elimination period is the time which must pass after filing a claim before a policyholder can collect insurance benefits.

○ You may have to put your insurance policy to use by filing a claim at some point.

fi|nan|cial ad|vis|er /faɪnænʃəl ədvaɪzər/ (**financial advisers**)

SALES AND DISTRIBUTION

NOUN A **financial adviser** is a life insurance and investment specialist who tells you how best to invest your money and protect your and your family's future.

○ *You should seek advice from a financial adviser to determine whether the life insurance policy in question is suitable for you.*

○ *If you are thinking about buying insurance protection, it is always a good idea to get expert help from an independent financial adviser.*

> **JOBS CONNECTED WITH INSURANCE**
>
> actuary, appraiser, average adjuster, financial adviser, financial underwriter, loss adjuster, risk manager, underwriter

fi|nan|cial un|der|writ|er /faɪnænʃəl ʌndərraɪtər/ (**financial underwriters**)

UNDERWRITING

NOUN A **financial underwriter** is an insurance employee working in financial underwriting.

○ *Financial underwriters are financial professionals who decide whether to grant insurance to organizations or individuals and determine the terms and cost of insurance plans based on risk factors.*

○ *The financial underwriter calculates the probability of something, and determines the premium to reflect that risk.*

fi|nan|cial un|der|writ|ing /faɪnænʃəl ʌndərraɪtɪŋ/

UNDERWRITING

NOUN **Financial underwriting** is the process of assessing whether the proposed sum insured and product are reasonable when considering the possible financial loss to the client.

○ *The high cost of the protection plus the difficulties in doing financial underwriting for large insurance policies will ensure that the maximum investments are kept in check.*

○ *Financial underwriting is the process of evaluating applicants for insurance and classifying them fairly so the appropriate premium rates may be charged.*

fire ex|tin|guish|er /faɪər ɪkstɪŋgwɪʃər/ (fire extinguishers)

RESIDENCE INSURANCE

NOUN A **fire extinguisher** is a metal container with water or chemicals in it, that is used for stopping small fires.

○ *Even small measures, such as keeping a fire extinguisher in your kitchen, will often qualify you for a discount on your premiums.*

○ *The insurance company determined that the fire extinguisher had not been properly maintained and was thus defective at the time the fire broke out.*

fire in|sur|ance /faɪər ɪnʃʊərəns/

COMMERCIAL INSURANCE

NOUN **Fire insurance** is insurance that pays money if your possessions are destroyed or damaged in a fire.

○ *In fire insurance, the physical hazards are analyzed according to the type of construction, exposure to other structures that may spread a conflagration, and type of occupancy.*

○ *Fire insurance is designed to indemnify the insured for loss of, or damage to, buildings and personal property by fire.*

first-loss pol|i|cy /fɜrst lɔs pɒlɪsi/ (first-loss policies)

REINSURANCE

NOUN A **first-loss policy** is an insurance policy for goods in which a total loss is unlikely and the insurer provides cover for a sum less than the total value of the goods.

○ *With large warehouses and stores where the value of stocks is considerable and of bulky nature rendering a full loss very unlikely, a first-loss policy may be given.*

○ *A first-loss policy is used when it is inconceivable that all property would be lost in a single claim.*

fleet in|sur|ance /fliːt ɪnʃʊərəns/

COMMERCIAL INSURANCE

NOUN **Fleet insurance** is a type of insurance contract that applies to a number of vehicles.

○ *A commercial fleet insurance company has warned that statistics show that those who use cellphones when driving are four times more likely to be involved in a collision.*

○ *Fleet insurance insures a group of vehicles, ships, or aircraft together under one policy.*

---

fleet rate /fliːt reɪt/ (fleet rates)

COMMERCIAL INSURANCE

NOUN A **fleet rate** is a reduced rate offered by an insurance company to underwrite the risks to a fleet of vehicles or aircraft.

○ *If your business grows to the point where the number of vehicles you have exceeds a certain number, your broker can negotiate a fleet rate.*

○ *A fleet rate is determined by assessing a group of vehicles, ships, or aircraft that are insured together under one policy.*

---

float|er /floʊtər/ (floaters)

RESIDENCE INSURANCE

NOUN A **floater** is an insurance policy that covers movable property, such as jewels or furs, regardless of where it is.

○ *Among the items often insured with a floater are expensive jewelry, musical instruments and furs.*

○ *A floater is available to cover the value of goods beyond the coverage of a standard renter's insurance policy including movable property such as jewelry or sports equipment.*

▶ SYNONYM:
  floating policy

---

flood /flʌd/ (floods)

RESIDENCE INSURANCE

NOUN If there is a **flood**, a large amount of water covers an area which is usually dry.

○ *Water damage from floods is covered under separate insurance policies issued by the federal government.*

○ *The flood risk of homeowners in floodplain areas is 26 times their fire risk.*

---

flood cov|er|age /flʌd kʌvərɪdʒ/

RESIDENCE INSURANCE

NOUN **Flood coverage** is insurance coverage for loss or damage caused by floods.

○ *Properties situated near the water should purchase excess flood coverage.*

○ *People living in flood-prone areas are generally required to buy flood coverage by their mortgage companies.*

---

forced place in|sur|ance /fɔrst pleɪs ɪnʃʊərəns/

COMMERCIAL INSURANCE

NOUN **Forced place insurance** is insurance taken out by a bank or creditor on an uninsured debtor's behalf on a property that is being used as collateral.

○ *Forced place insurance provides insurance coverage to protect the mortgage collateral against fire, flood, and other such property hazards.*

○ *When a mortgage company takes out forced place insurance, the only thing they are concerned with is whether or not the property in which they have a financial interest is covered.*

---

force ma|jeure /fɔrs mæʒɜr/

COMMERCIAL INSURANCE

NOUN **Force majeure** is an unexpected event, such as a war or an act of God, that prevents someone from doing what they had planned or agreed to do. From French, meaning "greater force."

○ *The defendants maintained that they were entitled to more time or money to perform their obligations as a result of the claimed force majeure event.*

○ *A declaration of force majeure refers to an inability to meet a contractual agreement because of forces beyond the shipper's control.*

---

fran|chise /fræntʃaɪz/ (**franchises**)

COMMERCIAL INSURANCE

NOUN In marine insurance, a **franchise** is a sum or percentage stated in a policy, below which the insurer does not have liability.

○ *Any loss below the franchise is met in its entirety by the insured.*

○ *A franchise is not a deductible percentage, but is the amount the claim must reach before the partial loss from a peril insured against is paid.*

fraud /frɔd/

GENERAL

NOUN Insurance **fraud** is the crime of gaining insurance benefits by being deliberately deceitful, dishonest, or untrue.

○ Insurance fraud ranges from completely fabricated claims, to inflation or padding of legitimate claims, to false statements on insurance applications.

○ Common types of insurance fraud are staged accidents, exaggerated injuries, and inflated medical bills.

fraud|u|lent /frɔdʒələnt/

GENERAL

ADJECTIVE A **fraudulent** act or insurance claim is deliberately deceitful, dishonest, or untrue.

○ A computerized register of information shared by insurance companies and the police helps to reduce fraudulent claims, which in turn, should help to keep everyone's premiums down.

○ The policy covers loss of property due to dishonest or fraudulent acts of one or more employees of the insured, resulting in improper financial gain.

front-end load /frʌnt ɛnd loʊd/ (**front-end loads**)

GENERAL

NOUN A **front-end load** is the charging of costs at the beginning of an insurance policy rather than spreading them over its term.

○ Replacement of an existing life insurance policy generally is not in the policy owner's best interest, as a new front-end load for commissions and expenses must be paid.

○ Variable annuities often come with substantial front-end loads as well as annual charges that run to about twice those of no-load funds.

F|S|A /ɛf ɛs eɪ/ (short for **Flexible Spending Account**)

MEDICAL INSURANCE

ABBREVIATION In the U.S., an **FSA** is an account that allows employees to set aside pretax income for routine medical expenses.

○ When you offer your employees a medical FSA, the plan reimburses participants for eligible health care expenses with pre-tax dollars.

○ *An FSA allows your employees to deduct pre-tax dollars to pay for qualified medical and dependent care expenses.*

---

fu|ner|al /fyu̱nərəl/ (funerals)

[LIFE INSURANCE]

NOUN A **funeral** is the ceremony held when the body of someone who has died is buried or cremated.

○ *This policy covers the costs of returning home to attend the funeral of a family member who has died.*

○ *The benefit is designed to contribute towards the cost of a funeral on the death of the insured person, by providing the nominated beneficiary with a lump sum payment.*

---

fu|ner|al ex|pens|es /fyu̱nərəl ikspɛnsɪz/

[LIFE INSURANCE]

NOUN **Funeral expenses** are the costs of organizing and carrying out a funeral.

○ *This type of insurance is designed specifically to cover funeral expenses when the insured person dies.*

○ *The widow or partner of the policyholder can get a portion of the benefit upfront for the funeral expenses until the full benefit is processed.*

---

fu|ner|al plan /fyu̱nərəl plæn/ (funeral plans)

[LIFE INSURANCE]

NOUN A **funeral plan** is a basic life insurance policy that provides money to pay for the policyholder's funeral expenses when they die.

○ *With our fully guaranteed funeral plan, you can pay ahead and beat inflation by freezing funeral costs at today's prices.*

○ *A funeral plan is a simple and straightforward way for people aged 50 or over to cover the cost of a funeral in advance and put arrangements in place.*

Gg

GAP in|sur|ance /gæp ɪnʃʊərəns/ (short for **Guaranteed Auto Protection insurance**)

VEHICLE INSURANCE

NOUN **GAP insurance** pays the difference between what someone owes on their car loan and the actual cash value of the vehicle in the event that it is stolen or damaged.

○ *GAP insurance policies are often offered at auto dealerships as a comparatively low cost add-on to the car loan that provides coverage for the duration of the loan.*

○ *GAP insurance covers the difference between a car's actual cash value when it is stolen or wrecked and the amount the consumer owes the leasing or finance company.*

gate|keep|er /geɪtkiːpər/ (**gatekeepers**)

GENERAL

NOUN A **gatekeeper** is a set of requirements for a long-term care insurance policy that a policyholder must meet to qualify for benefits.

○ *A gatekeeper could require a doctor to certify that a person is unable to perform certain daily living activities.*

○ *Gatekeeper provisions in long-term care policies determine whether an individual will qualify for benefits.*

WORD BUILDER

-er = person, organization, or thing that does something

The suffix **-er** often appears in words for things that have a particular purpose: **binder**, **floater**, **gatekeeper**, **waiver**.

It also appears frequently in words for people or organizations that do particular things: **appraiser**, **insurer**, **proposer**, **underwriter**.

---

gen|der /dʒɛndər/

UNDERWRITING

NOUN **Gender** is the state of being male or female.

- o *The three main variables in a mortality table are age, gender, and use of tobacco.*
- o *For auto insurance, gender is taken into consideration, as statistically, males have more accidents than females.*

gen|er|al av|er|age /dʒɛnərəl ævərɪdʒ/

COMMERCIAL INSURANCE: MARINE INSURANCE

NOUN **General average** is loss or damage to a ship or its cargo that is shared among the owners of the ship and cargo.

- o *A general average loss falls on all parties to the voyage.*
- o *General average is proportioned among all of the parties to the marine voyage, including the various owners of the cargo and the vessel owner.*

gen|er|al in|sur|ance /dʒɛnərəl ɪnʃʊərəns/

GENERAL

NOUN **General insurance** is insurance coverage for property and liability risks.

- o *With general insurance, payments made by insurance companies are based on the loss incurred, rather than being a fixed sum as in life insurance.*
- o *Exclusions are items or conditions that are not covered by the general insurance contract.*

good driv|er dis|count /gʊd draɪvər dɪskaʊnt/ (**good driver discounts**)

VEHICLE INSURANCE

NOUN A **good driver discount** is a discount on insurance that is available to drivers who have no at-fault accidents and no traffic offenses during a particular period.

- o *Most insurance companies give people with clear driving records a good driver discount of 20 percent to 25 percent.*
- o *Many companies give good driver discounts if you have not been convicted of a moving violation or been in an accident over the term of the policy.*

gross pre|mi|um /grəʊs prɪmiəm/ (**gross premiums**)

SALES AND DISTRIBUTION

NOUN A **gross premium** is the total premium of an insurance contract before brokerage or discounts have been deducted.

○ In reinsurance, the primary insurance company usually pays the reinsurer its proportion of the gross premium it receives on a risk.

○ The gross premium is the total premium paid by the policy owner, and generally consists of the net premium plus the expense of operation minus interest.

gross writ|ten pre|mi|ums /grəʊs rɪtᵊn prɪmiəmz/

SALES AND DISTRIBUTION

NOUN **Gross written premiums** are the total revenue from a contract expected to be received by an insurer before deductions for reinsurance or ceding commissions.

○ Surplus gains enabled the company to increase gross written premiums and reduce amounts ceded to reinsurers.

○ Gross written premiums are premiums with no deduction of the cost of any reinsurance or any adjustment for the fact that some of the income has to be reserved for the unexpired element of the policy.

group in|sur|ance /gruːp ɪnʃʊərəns/

LIFE INSURANCE

NOUN **Group insurance** is life, health, or accident insurance which covers several people, especially employees of a company, under a single contract at reduced premiums.

○ Many group insurance plans require that there must be a minimum number of persons covered, such as 10 or 25.

○ The group insurance market consists mainly of employers who arrange group contracts to cover their employees.

Hh

---

haz|ard /ˈhæzərd/ (hazards)

NOUN A **hazard** is something that increases the possibility or size of a loss.

- ○ *The storing of explosives in a home basement is a hazard that increases the probability of an explosion.*

- ○ *Coverage is provided for a wide range of hazards including theft, weather, fire, and collision.*

---

health in|sur|ance ex|change (ABBR HIX)
/ˈhɛlθ ɪnˈʃʊərəns ɪksˈtʃeɪndʒ/ (**health insurance exchanges**)

MEDICAL INSURANCE

NOUN A **health insurance exchange** is a set of health care plans in the U.S. from which people may purchase insurance that is eligible for federal subsidies.

- ○ *The taxpayer must be covered by a qualified health plan bought through a state health insurance exchange.*

- ○ *Health insurance exchanges are the central mechanisms created by the health reform bill to help individuals and small businesses purchase health insurance coverage.*

---

health main|te|nance or|gan|i|za|tion (ABBR HMO)
/ˈhɛlθ ˈmeɪntənəns ˌɔrgənɪˈzeɪʃən/ (**health maintenance organizations**)

MEDICAL INSURANCE

NOUN A **health maintenance organization** is an organization providing health care coverage in the U.S. that is carried out by hospitals, doctors, and other providers with which it has a contract.

○ *A health maintenance organization may issue a contract that limits coverage to home health care services only.*

○ *A health maintenance organization is a health delivery system consisting of health providers where members pay a premium for which medical care is received when needed.*

---

health main|te|nance plan /hɛlθ meɪntənəns plæn/
(health maintenance plans)

MEDICAL INSURANCE

NOUN A **health maintenance plan** is a health insurance policy that provides preventive care like vaccinations, doctor checkups, and screenings, for a prepaid fee.

○ *The purpose of a health maintenance plan is to find and treat medical conditions before they become serious and more expensive.*

○ *The emphasis of a health maintenance plan is on preventive medicine, and it is an alternative to employee benefit plans.*

---

health ques|tion|naire /hɛlθ kwɛstʃənɛər/ (health questionnaires)

MEDICAL INSURANCE

NOUN A **health questionnaire** is a list of questions about someone's health issued by underwriters before accepting a person as a risk.

○ *Failure to volunteer full information on a health questionnaire can result in coverage being voided during a claim.*

○ *If the health questionnaire reveals that you have been treated for a certain disease, such as cancer or heart disease, the insurer may add a rider to the policy that excludes the condition.*

---

high-de|duct|i|ble health plan (ABBR HDHP)
/haɪ dɪdʌktɪbəl hɛlθ plæn/ (high-deductible health plans)

MEDICAL INSURANCE

NOUN In the U.S., a **high-deductible health plan** is a health insurance plan with lower premiums and higher deductibles than usual.

○ *Monthly premium costs for the high-deductible health plan option will be lower than the cost of standard health plans.*

○ *By enrolling in a high-deductible health plan, the participant pays lower insurance premiums than they otherwise would with traditional health insurance.*

high-risk /haɪ rɪsk/

GENERAL

ADJECTIVE A **high-risk** customer, risk, occupation, or property is particularly likely to be exposed to a danger.

- *Certain types of occupations, which are more physically intensive or expose the person to hazardous work environments, are considered high-risk type occupations.*
- *This policy is a way of providing automobile insurance to persons considered to be high-risk drivers who cannot obtain protection in the voluntary markets.*

> **RELATED WORDS**
>
> A customer may be high-risk because of **adverse selection**, the tendency of those in dangerous jobs or with high-risk lifestyles to want to take out life insurance. These customers may have a high level of **occupational hazard**.
>
> The opposite of high-risk is **low-risk**.

HIP|AA /hɪpə/ (short for **Health Insurance Portability and Accountability Act**)

MEDICAL INSURANCE

ABBREVIATION In the U.S., **HIPAA** is an act that protects people covered by health insurance and makes rules about storing personal medical data.

- *Internal audits play a key role in HIPAA compliance by reviewing operations with the goal of identifying potential security violations.*
- *The HIPAA guarantees that employers are not able to impose pre-existing condition limitations in the insurance they offer to new employees.*

hit and run /hɪt ᵊnd rʌn/ (**hit and runs**)

VEHICLE INSURANCE

NOUN A **hit and run** is an accident in which a car driver hits someone and does not stop to help.

- *The term "uninsured motorist" includes someone who cannot be identified, such as the driver in a hit and run.*

○ *You do not lose your entitlement to access compensation because you are the victim of a hit and run even if the vehicle could not be identified, or if it was unregistered.*

---

home in|sur|ance /hoʊm ɪnʃʊərəns/

RESIDENCE INSURANCE

NOUN **Home insurance** is insurance coverage for your home, its contents, and your possessions.

○ *Some streets seem to attract crime more than others, so the suburb or even the street you live in can affect your home insurance premiums.*

○ *Most home insurance policies provide additional living expenses that will pay some expenses if your home is damaged by an insured event to the extent that you cannot live there while repairs are being made.*

> **TYPES OF INSURANCE**
>
> The following are all types of insurance that people take out to protect buildings, land, and possessions in their homes:
>
> earthquake coverage, flood coverage, real estate insurance, renter's insurance, replacement cost insurance, residence insurance

---

home|own|er /hoʊmoʊnər/ (homeowners)

RESIDENCE INSURANCE

NOUN A **homeowner** is a person who owns a house, or owns the house or apartment that they live in.

○ *This policy is the most commonly written policy for a homeowner, and is designed to cover all aspects of the home, structure, and its contents.*

○ *Most homeowner policies contain replacement cost coverage on the home and actual cash value coverage on personal property.*

H|R|A /eɪtʃ ɑr eɪ/ (short for **health reimbursement account**)

MEDICAL INSURANCE

ABBREVIATION In the U.S., an **HRA** is a program that allows an employer to set aside funds to reimburse medical expenses paid by participating employees.

○An HRA lets you set aside a specific amount of pre-tax dollars for employees to pay for health care expenses on an annual basis.

○As the employer, you establish the medical expenses for which the HRA funds may be used.

H|S|A /eɪtʃ ɛs eɪ/ (short for **health savings account**)

MEDICAL INSURANCE

ABBREVIATION In the U.S., an **HSA** is a medical savings account with tax advantages that is available to taxpayers who are enrolled in a high deductible health plan.

○You cannot be enrolled in Medicare or be a dependent on another person's tax return to qualify for an HSA.

○With a high-deductible health plan, money contributed to the HSA account is considered pre-tax, and therefore works to reduce the insured's income taxes.

---

hur|ri|cane /hɜrɪkeɪn/ (**hurricanes**)

COMMERCIAL INSURANCE

NOUN A **hurricane** is an extremely violent storm that begins over ocean water.

○These ratings are used to give an estimate of the potential property damage and flooding expected along the coast from a hurricane.

○Certain risks can't obtain coverage in the voluntary market such as coastal properties subject to hurricanes.

Ii

im|me|di|ate an|nu|i|ty /ɪmidiɪt ɪnuɪti/ (**immediate annuities**)

LIFE INSURANCE

NOUN An **immediate annuity** is an annuity contract in which payouts begin immediately or within one year.

- ○ An immediate annuity allows you to turn a one-time lump sum payment into a guaranteed series of payouts that generally begin within a year of the annuity issue date.
- ○ An immediate annuity is purchased for a single premium or lump sum, and provides an immediate income to the annuitant.

im|pair|ment /ɪmpɛərmənt/ (**impairments**)

MEDICAL INSURANCE

NOUN An **impairment** is a condition in which a part of a person's mind or body is damaged or is not working properly.

- ○ A person with a disability is defined as a person who has a physical or mental impairment that substantially limits one or more major life activities.
- ○ Enhanced annuities are likely to be weighted towards exposure to a handful of impairments, particularly cardiovascular disease and conditions related to smoking.

in|cep|tion /ɪnsɛpʃən/

LIFE INSURANCE

NOUN The **inception** of a risk or a policy is the date when it started and when it started to be covered.

- ○ If the contract owner withdraws more than a certain specified amount within a specified number of years since inception of the policy, most insurance companies will impose an early-withdrawal penalty.

◦ *The initial premium is the amount paid at the inception of an insurance contract, usually subject to adjustment at the end of the policy period.*

---

in|come pro|tec|tion in|sur|ance /ɪnkʌm prətɛkʃən ɪnʃʊərəns/

MEDICAL INSURANCE

NOUN **Income protection insurance** is a type of health insurance that compensates someone for part of the income that they lose because of illness or injury that prevents them from working.

◦ *If you are injured and are unable to continue working, income protection insurance will enable you to pay debts and maintain an adequate standard of living.*

◦ *With an unemployment income protection insurance policy behind you, at least when it comes to financial matters such as your mortgage and other payments there will not be a problem.*

---

in|dem|ni|ty /ɪndɛmnɪti/

GENERAL

NOUN **Indemnity** is compensation for damage or loss.

◦ *In case of loss of the vessel, the ship owner receives no indemnity for loss, but acquires immunity from payment of the loan.*

◦ *The policy may pay certain or all expenses for medical and similar services and a weekly or monthly indemnity for loss of income.*

---

in|dem|ni|ty plan /ɪndɛmnɪti plæn/ (**indemnity plans**)

MEDICAL INSURANCE

NOUN An **indemnity plan** is a healthcare plan that allows policyholders to choose any healthcare provider they wish, and charges them a fee depending on the rules of the policy.

◦ *The indemnity plan, even though more costly, would provide the patient with the greatest number of choices among physicians and hospitals.*

◦ *Under a traditional group indemnity plan, an insured can bypass a primary care physician and see a specialist directly.*

in|dex /ˈɪndɛks/ (**indexes**)

⌐LIFE INSURANCE¬

NOUN An **index** is a system by which prices and costs can be compared to those of a previous date.

○ *The level of coverage increases in line with an index of prices or earnings.*

○ *Benefits are increased at periodic intervals by a factor derived from an index of prices or earnings.*

in|dex-linked /ˈɪndɛks lɪŋkt/

⌐LIFE INSURANCE: PENSIONS¬

ADJECTIVE **Index-linked** wages, pensions, or insurance policies increase or decrease according to the rise or fall of prices.

○ *Not all policies will be index-linked, so add a suitable allowance for inflation during the lifetime of the policy.*

○ *An index-linked pension delivers annual increases linked to inflation.*

in|fla|tion rid|er /ɪnˈfleɪʃᵊn raɪdər/ (**inflation riders**)

⌐LIFE INSURANCE: PENSIONS¬

NOUN An **inflation rider** is a rider that can be added to a long-term care insurance plan that adjusts the benefits over time to allow for inflation.

○ *Inflation riders can adjust benefits annually based on a simple or compound fixed rate, or based on the consumer price index.*

○ *The inflation rider option increases benefits according to a stated index each year after benefits begin to be paid.*

in|i|tial com|mis|sion /ɪnɪʃᵊl kəmɪʃᵊn/

⌐SALES AND DISTRIBUTION¬

NOUN **Initial commission** is commission that is paid to someone who sells or recommends a financial product for the first time.

○ *On an introduction of business to the insurer, the agent is typically paid an upfront initial commission to reward both the prospecting costs and the sales effort.*

○ *After the successful sale of an insurance product, regardless of the specific type of policy, the agent who is responsible for acquiring the new client and closing the deal will be paid an initial commission.*

RELATED WORDS

Compare **initial commission** with a **trail commission**, that is a further commission of between 0.1 and 1 percent that is paid to an adviser provided that the client's funds remain invested in the product for a specified time.

in|pa|tient /ɪnpeɪʃ^ənt/ (inpatients)

MEDICAL INSURANCE

NOUN An **inpatient** is someone who stays in a hospital while they receive treatment.

○ If a given condition can be treated equally well as an outpatient than as an inpatient, cost savings will generally be realized.

○ A healthcare professional will evaluate an attending physician's request for a patient's admission to a hospital to evaluate whether or not inpatient care is necessary.

in|sti|tu|tion /ɪnstɪtuʃ^ən/ (institutions)

GENERAL

NOUN An **institution** is a large organization such as an insurance company or a bank that has large sums of money to invest on a stock exchange.

○ The financial crisis shook many people's confidence in the institutions that traditionally provided guarantees or insurance against such events.

○ Insurance products shift the responsibility of providing lifetime income from the individual to the institution selling the product, typically insurance companies.

in|sur|a|bil|i|ty /ɪnʃʊərəbɪlɪti/

GENERAL

NOUN A person's **insurability** is how acceptable they are to an insurer as an applicant for insurance.

○ A medical examination must be given by a qualified physician to determine the insurability of an applicant.

○ The amount of insurance may be automatically increased, without evidence of insurability, at predetermined periods for a maximum amount.

in|sur|a|ble /ɪnʃʊərəbᵊl/

GENERAL

ADJECTIVE If property or a risk are **insurable**, you are able to get insurance for them.

○ In order to be insurable, the risk insured against must meet certain characteristics.

○ One of the conditions that make a risk insurable is that the loss must be calculable and the cost of insuring it must be economically feasible.

in|sur|a|ble in|ter|est /ɪnʃʊərəbᵊl ɪntrɪst/

GENERAL

NOUN If a person has an **insurable interest** in the life or property covered by an insurance contract, they would suffer financial loss if the thing insured were damaged or destroyed.

○ In property insurance, the beneficiary is required to have an insurable interest in the property insured.

○ You may not take out insurance on an object or a life in which you have no insurable interest.

in|sur|ance¹ /ɪnʃʊərəns/

GENERAL

NOUN **Insurance** is an arrangement in which you pay money to a company, and they provide financial protection for your property, life, or health, paying you in case of death, loss, or damage.

○ For insurance purposes the word "disability" will have a special and particular meaning which will be defined in the policy concerned.

○ Often the person arranging your insurance will charge fees as well as receiving a commission.

in|sur|ance² /ɪnʃʊərəns/

GENERAL

NOUN **Insurance** is a policy that provides financial protection for your property, life, or health, paying you in case of death, loss, or damage.

○ Before buying insurance, make sure that the coverage provided exactly suits your needs.

○ Uninsured motorists coverage pays for costs resulting from an accident involving a hit-and-run driver or a driver who does not have insurance.

in|sur|ance³ /ɪnʃʊərəns/

GENERAL

NOUN Insurance is the financial amount of protection that you receive for your property, life, or health in case of death, loss, or damage.

○ *You should check the dollar limits of insurance in your policy, and make sure you are comfortable with the amount of coverage you have for specific items.*

○ *Full coverage covers all losses, with no deductions, up to the amount of the insurance.*

in|sur|ance a|gent (ABBR **agent**) /ɪnʃʊərəns eɪdʒªnt/
(**insurance agents**)

SALES AND DISTRIBUTION

NOUN An **insurance agent** is a representative of an insurer who negotiates and sells insurance contracts.

○ *The amount of insurance a property owner needs should be discussed with an insurance agent.*

○ *Coverage for flood damage is sold by licensed insurance agents.*

in|sur|ance bro|ker (ABBR **broker**) /ɪnʃʊərəns broʊkər/
(**insurance brokers**)

SALES AND DISTRIBUTION

NOUN An **insurance broker** is someone who advises people on their insurance needs and negotiates insurance contracts on their behalf with insurers in return for a fee or commission.

○ *We paid an insurance broker to look for insurance on our behalf.*

○ *Insurance brokers act as middlemen between firms that want to insure their property and casualty risks and the insurers that underwrite policies.*

in|sur|ance class /ɪnʃʊərəns klæs/ (**insurance classes**)

GENERAL

NOUN An **insurance class** is a type of insurance coverage such as liability, health, legal expenses, or construction risk.

○ *Premiums for health insurance constitute only a small part of the overall premiums for the accident and health insurance class.*

○ *A combination of factors has hampered the development of the property insurance class, including low disposable incomes and a high proportion of individuals in rented accommodations.*

---

in|sur|ance sales|man (insurance saleswoman, insurance salesperson) /ɪnʃʊərəns seɪlzmən/ (insurance salesmen)

[SALES AND DISTRIBUTION]

NOUN An **insurance salesman** is an employee of an insurance company whose job is to advise on and sell insurance.

○ *You are unlikely to obtain the most coverage for your premium dollar if you rely on the advice of only one insurance salesman.*

○ *There is no fixed rule about how much commission an insurance salesman makes on a typical business policy.*

---

in|sure /ɪnʃʊər/ (insures, insured, insuring)

[GENERAL]

VERB If a company **insures** you or your property, they issue you an insurance policy.

○ *For protection against unforeseen emergencies, you insure your house, your furnishings, and your car.*

○ *Coverage does not apply to aircraft or watercraft, which must be separately insured.*

---

in|sured¹ /ɪnʃʊərd/

[GENERAL]

ADJECTIVE An **insured** item or person is covered by insurance.

○ *Auto insurance coverage provides protection in the event of physical damage to, or theft of, the insured car.*

○ *An example of bodily injury is where an insured driver causes bodily harm to a third party and is deemed responsible for the injuries.*

---

in|sured² /ɪnʃʊərd/ (insureds)

[GENERAL]

NOUN An **insured** is a person or organization covered by an insurance policy.

○ The payments made while the insured is living are deducted from any death benefits paid to beneficiaries.

○ If your mother applies for and is issued a policy on your life, then she is the policy owner and you are the insured.

---

in|sur|er /ɪnʃʊərər/ (**insurers**)

GENERAL

NOUN An **insurer** is a company that sells insurance.

○ The insurer pays the insured the cash value which the policy has built up if it is surrendered.

○ It is mandatory for insurers to provide the customers with a prospectus that carries all the major features of the policy.

RELATED WORDS

A **coinsurer** is a person or company whose policy covers the same risk as that of another person or company, and shares the loss.

A **direct insurer** is an insurance company that sells its policies directly to customers without using intermediaries.

A **mutual insurer** is an insurance company which is owned by its members or policyholders rather than by shareholders.

A **primary insurer** is the insurance company that first sells insurance to a client, who later purchases reinsurance.

A **reinsurer** is an insurance company that insures the risks of other insurance companies.

---

in|ter|me|di|ar|y /ɪntərmiːdiɛri/ (**intermediaries**)

SALES AND DISTRIBUTION

NOUN An **intermediary** is someone such as an agent or broker through whom insurance contracts are arranged between a customer and an insurance company.

○ An intermediary helps companies find appropriate coverage, and can arrange for sufficient insurance from multiple insurers if no single insurance company will accept the entire risk.

○ An intermediary negotiates reinsurance contracts between the ceding company and the reinsurer.

in|vest|ment bond /ɪnvɛstmənt bɒnd/ (**investment bonds**)

LIFE INSURANCE

NOUN An **investment bond** is a single-premium life insurance policy in which a fixed sum is invested in an asset-backed fund (= a financial organization that invests in property or shares.)

○ With an investment bond, you invest a lump sum with an insurance company and get a little bit of life coverage, but the rest is invested.

○ Investment bonds are popular investment plans sold by a life insurance company, whereby investors pay in a lump sum which is invested in one or more collective funds.

I|R|S /aɪ ɑr ɛs/ (short for **Internal Revenue Service**)

GENERAL

ABBREVIATION The **IRS** is the part of the U.S. Department of the Treasury that is responsible for collecting taxes.

○ If you cancel your annuity, 10 percent penalty on the taxable portion of the annuity is forfeited to the IRS if you are under age 59.

○ The higher your income the more attractive your return becomes to the IRS.

---

is|sue a pol|i|cy /ɪʃu ə pɒlɪsi/ (**issues a policy, issued a policy, issuing a policy**)

GENERAL

PHRASE If an insurer **issues a policy**, they create an insurance policy and provide it to a customer.

○ Your application is used by the insurance company to decide whether or not to issue a policy.

○ For us to issue a policy, the correct premium payment must accompany the application.

Jj

joint life an|nu|i|ty /dʒɔɪnt laɪf ənuɪti/ (joint life annuities)

LIFE INSURANCE: PENSIONS

NOUN A **joint life annuity** is a life insurance policy that pays a benefit that continues throughout the joint lifetime of two people until one of them dies.

○ *A joint life annuity guarantees income for you and your spouse for as long as you or your spouse live.*

○ *In order to protect the survivors of the retired person, a joint life annuity, which is a life annuity payable to the last survivor of two or more people, can be selected.*

key man in|sur|ance /kɪ mæn ɪnʃʊərəns/

COMMERCIAL INSURANCE

NOUN **Key man insurance** is an insurance policy taken out by a small company on the life of a senior executive whose death would create a serious loss.

- *A consideration applicable to business owners is key man insurance for the person or people essential to your business operations.*

- *Key man insurance could help your business get through a period where a director or top salesman was critically ill and could not work for months, or perhaps was forced to retire.*

land|slide /ˈlændslaɪd/ (landslides)

NOUN A **landslide** is a large amount of earth or rocks falling down a hill, cliff, or the side of a mountain.

- ○ *Damage caused by earth movement, whether by earthquake, landslide, or volcanic eruption, is covered up to the stated policy limit with a deductible.*

- ○ *The policy does not cover earth movements, such as landslides, in which damage is caused by movement of actual elements of the ground, including rocks, trees, and parts of houses.*

lapse¹ /ˈlæps/ (lapses)

NOUN A **lapse** is a failure to renew a policy by the policyholder or the insurer.

- ○ *Renewal notices are sent approximately 45 days prior to your present license expiration date, and it is the responsibility of each licensee to ensure that their licenses are current and there is no lapse.*

- ○ *As long as the policy is renewed annually without lapse, the amount of premium payable for all future terms will be maintained at the same level.*

lapse² /ˈlæps/ (lapses)

NOUN A **lapse** is the termination of a policy because the insurer does not invite the policyholder to renew, or because the policyholder does not pay the premiums.

- ○ *Insurers may ask if you have previously had insurance coverage, because they want to know if you have ever had a policy canceled for non-payment of premiums, causing a lapse in coverage.*

- ○ *The reinstatement may be effective after the cancellation date, creating a lapse of coverage.*

leak|age /ˈliːkɪdʒ/

CLAIMS

NOUN **Leakage** is premium revenue that is lost, often because a policyholder has not been truthful about facts or lifestyle changes or has committed some fraud.

○ *Leakage arising from fraud, poor claims procedures, or simply from lack of proper control procedures costs insurers millions of dollars every year.*

○ *In an ideal world, insurers would reduce claims leakage to zero, but some cases, due to fraudulent claims, are unavoidable.*

le|gal ex|pens|es in|sur|ance /ˈliːɡəl ɪksˈpɛnsɪz ɪnˈʃʊərəns/

GENERAL

NOUN **Legal expenses insurance** is insurance coverage against expenses incurred when you need to seek legal advice or pay for a lawsuit.

○ *Regulations for legal expenses insurance state that, under such a policy, the insured person has the right to choose his own lawyer.*

○ *There may be occasions when you simply have to use the courts to stand up for yourself, and this is when a legal expenses insurance policy can be a great help.*

lev|el pre|mi|um term in|sur|ance /ˈlɛvəl ˈpriːmiəm tɜːrm ɪnˈʃʊərəns/

LIFE INSURANCE

NOUN **Level premium term insurance** is term insurance with premiums that remain the same throughout the life of the contract.

○ *With level premium term insurance, the amount of the level premium is higher than needed for the protection provided in the early years of the contract but less than needed in the later years.*

○ *Level premium term insurance guarantees your premium will stay the same each year for the term of your policy, generally 5 to 20 years.*

li|a|bil|i|ty /ˌlaɪəˈbɪlɪti/ (liabilities)

GENERAL

NOUN **Liability** is legal responsibility for paying money for damage or injury.

○ The policy also provides personal liability coverage for damage the policyholder or dependents cause to third parties.

○ An adjuster will determine the extent of the insurer's liability for loss when a claim is submitted.

---

li|a|ble /ˈlaɪəbᵊl/

GENERAL

ADJECTIVE If you are **liable** for something, you are legally responsible for paying the cost of it.

○ Travelers who are not covered by insurance are personally liable for covering incurred medical and associated costs.

○ The face amount of a policy is the amount for which it is written and, therefore, the limit the insurer may be liable to pay in one loss.

▶ COLLOCATION:
liable for

---

life in|sur|ance (BRIT **life assurance**) /ˈlaɪf ɪnˈʃʊərəns/

LIFE INSURANCE

NOUN **Life insurance** is insurance that pays a sum of money to you after a period of time, or to your family when you die.

○ With many life insurance policies, the only benefit received is a lump sum payout on death.

○ An accidental death benefit is a provision that may be added to a life insurance policy which provides payment of an additional benefit in the case of death resulting from an accident.

---

life ta|ble /ˈlaɪf teɪbᵊl/ (**life tables**)

LIFE INSURANCE

NOUN A **life table** is a table showing how many deaths occur at specified ages, that insurance companies use to determine the life expectancy of insureds.

○ A life table shows, for each age, what the probability is that a person of that age will die before his or her next birthday.

○ A life table follows a group of individuals and records the number of deaths for each age group over a period of time.

life|time lim|it /ˈlaɪftaɪm lɪmɪt/ (**lifetime limits**)

MEDICAL INSURANCE

NOUN The **lifetime limit** of a health insurance plan is the maximum coverage that it offers, after which payment stops, and the policyholder must pay all remaining costs.

○ *Instead of using a per claim maximum, most insurers write a lifetime limit on medical policies.*

○ *Approximately 55% of individuals with employer-provided health insurance are subject to lifetime limits; the most common of which are $1 million and $2 million.*

light|ning /ˈlaɪtnɪŋ/

RESIDENCE INSURANCE

NOUN **Lightning** is electrical discharges causing very bright flashes of light in the sky and often, when striking the ground, causing severe damage to persons or objects.

○ *Fire insurance is coverage protecting property against losses caused by a fire or lightning.*

○ *When his boat, which also doubles as his home, was struck by lightning, the insurance company refused to pay out.*

line /laɪn/ (**lines**)

UNDERWRITING

NOUN A **line** is the amount of a risk that an underwriter is prepared to accept.

○ *Insurance companies have line limits, or maximum amounts of insurance they will write on any given submission.*

○ *The net line is the amount of insurance that an insurance company carries on a risk and retains for its own account.*

line of busi|ness /laɪn əv bɪznɪs/ (**lines of business**)

GENERAL

NOUN A **line of business** is a general classification of business used by the insurance industry, such as fire, commercial, personal, auto, or residence.

○ *Property and casualty insurers currently make the most money from their auto insurance line of business.*

○ *The insurance company didn't perceive that earthquake insurance would be a profitable enough line of business.*

Lloyd's of Lon|don /lɔɪdz əv lʌndən/

GENERAL

NOUN **Lloyd's of London** is an association of London underwriters which originally specialized in marine insurance but now provides a variety of insurance policies.

○ *Originally begun to insure the safe passage of ships, today Lloyd's of London takes in just under 3 percent of all insurance premiums worldwide.*

○ *Lloyd's of London is not an insurance company, but an incorporated association of insurers that specializes in marine insurance.*

---

load /loʊd/ (loads, loaded, loading)

UNDERWRITING

VERB If an insurer **loads** a premium, they increase it to cover expenses or an extra risk.

○ *Where you have an existing injury, the company will load your premium or totally exclude that injured part of your body.*

○ *Some insurers load the premium by 50 percent for those over 60, while others charge normal rates, recognizing that this group tends to be more careful and experienced.*

---

load|ing /loʊdɪŋ/ (loadings)

UNDERWRITING

NOUN A **loading** is an addition to an insurance premium to cover expenses or an extra risk.

○ *A loading or exclusion will be added to people from a risk group with higher or extra mortality.*

○ *Using self-insurance eliminates the various loadings such as acquisition expenses, taxes, and general expenses that would be incurred if the same loss coverage were secured through an insurance company.*

lon|gev|i|ty /lɒndʒɛvɪti/

MEDICAL INSURANCE

NOUN **Longevity** is the amount of time that someone lives.

○ *Quantifying the economic value of improved health and greater expected longevity is difficult.*

○ *Since women have greater longevity than men, they will need more in savings to cover health care insurance premiums and out-of-pocket expenses in retirement.*

lon|gev|i|ty risk /lɒndʒɛvɪti rɪsk/ (**longevity risks**)

LIFE INSURANCE

NOUN **Longevity risk** is the potential risk attached to the increasing life expectancy of policyholders, which can result in higher than expected payouts for insurance companies.

○ *Longer life expectancies lead to increased longevity risk for insurance companies that have made guarantees based on the entire lifetime of individuals.*

○ *Insurance institutions have always specialized in understanding and managing mortality and longevity risk.*

long-tail claims /lɒŋ teɪl kleɪmz/

LIFE INSURANCE

NOUN **Long-tail claims** are claims that are made or settled a long time after the insurance policy has expired.

○ *Because the insurance company is responsible only for claims made while the policy is in force, no long-tail claims problem occurs.*

○ *Common long-tail claims that arise after a long delay for employers may be claims for damages from situations such as asbestosis or noise induced hearing loss.*

RELATED WORDS

Compare with **short-tail business**, where it is known that claims will be made and settled quickly.

---

long-term care in|sur|ance /lɔŋ tɜrm kɛər ɪnʃʊərəns/

NOUN **Long-term care insurance** is insurance for people who may require long-term health or nursing care, and pays for things such as nursing homes and adult day care.

○ *If you have a long-term care insurance policy, the benefits will be triggered when you begin to need help with activities of daily living or have a severe cognitive impairment.*

○ *A long-term care insurance policy provides money to help cover the costs of living if you are no longer able to take care of yourself.*

loss¹ /lɔs/ (**losses**)

NOUN A **loss** is a situation in which something happens that has been insured against, which causes a policyholder to make a claim.

○ *Large firms often self-insure frequent, small losses such as damage to their fleet of vehicles or minor workplace injuries.*

○ *An insurable risk is a risk where the loss insured against is capable of being defined.*

loss² /lɔs/ (**losses**)

NOUN A **loss** is the amount of the claim when something happens that has been insured against.

○ *In this insurance clause, the policyholder pays for the deductible plus 20 percent of his covered losses.*

○ *After paying 80 percent of losses up to a specified ceiling, the insurer starts paying 100 percent.*

loss ad|just|er (ABBR **adjuster**) /lɔs ədʒʌstər/ (**loss adjusters**)

NOUN A **loss adjuster** is a person who is employed by an insurance company to evaluate an insurance claim and decide how much money should be paid to a person making a claim.

○ *The insurer will send an insurance loss adjuster to assess the damage to your vehicle, after which the insurer will authorize repairs.*

○ *Your demand letter should provide the loss adjuster with the information required to evaluate your claim.*

---

loss ra|ti|o /lɒs reɪʃoʊ/ (**loss ratios**)

[GENERAL]

NOUN A **loss ratio** is the amount of money that an insurance company pays out in one year, divided by the amount of money that it receives in premiums.

○ *A loss ratio expresses the relationship between insured losses and premiums.*

○ *The loss ratio is incurred losses and loss-adjustment expenses divided by net earned premium.*

---

low-risk /loʊ rɪsk/

[UNDERWRITING]

ADJECTIVE A **low-risk** customer, risk, occupation, or property is not very likely to be exposed to a danger.

○ *Expect to pay more for a policy that covers a high-risk occupation compared to a low-risk line of work.*

○ *Preferred market auto insurance features the lowest premiums, and is available to low-risk drivers with exceptional driving records.*

---

lump sum pay|ment /lʌmp sʌm peɪmənt/ (**lump sum payments**)

[LIFE INSURANCE]

NOUN A **lump sum payment** is an amount of money that is paid in one single payment rather than in installments.

○ *Life insurance policies provide either a lump sum payment or a set annual amount for a fixed period.*

○ *Rather than an annuity, retirees in poor health may derive greater benefit from a lump sum payment.*

Mm

---

make a pol|i|cy paid up /meɪk ə pɒlɪsi peɪd ʌp/ (**makes a policy paid up, made a policy paid up, making a policy paid up**)

LIFE INSURANCE

PHRASE If you **make a policy paid up**, you stop making premium payments into a life policy but still leave the coverage in place.

○ If you stop paying premiums after 3 years, you have the option to make the policy paid up, provided the policy has accumulated sufficient policy value.

○ If endowment policyholders make their policy paid up, the life cover will still continue and pay out if one of them passed away, but the insurer will reduce the amount of the guaranteed sum for which they are insured.

---

ma|li|cious dam|age /məlɪʃəs dæmɪdʒ/

RESIDENCE INSURANCE

NOUN **Malicious damage** is damage caused on purpose to the property of another person.

○ Crime insurance protects businesses from theft and malicious damage, such as employee embezzlement.

○ The policy defined vandalism as "malicious damage to, or destruction of the described property."

▶ **SYNONYM:**
malicious mischief

---

man|age a risk /mænɪdʒ ə rɪsk/ (**manages a risk, managed a risk, managing a risk**)

GENERAL

PHRASE If you **manage a risk**, you analyze how much you are in danger from a particular risk or hazard, and decide how to best deal with it.

○ Farmers use crop insurance to reduce or manage risks associated with growing crops.

○ *For most insurance and reinsurance companies whose expertise is in understanding and managing risks, market movements are typically the largest sources of uncertainty.*

---

ma|rine in|sur|ance /mərin ɪnʃʊərəns/

COMMERCIAL INSURANCE

NOUN **Marine insurance** is insurance that covers damage to shipping and cargo.

○ *Freight insurance is a common coverage in marine insurance, purchased by the owners of transporting vessels.*

○ *Historically, ocean marine insurance held the transporter responsible for property loss before, during, and after the completion of the voyage.*

---

ma|ture¹ /mətʃʊər/ (matures, matured, maturing)

LIFE INSURANCE

VERB If a financial arrangement such as a bond or an insurance policy **matures**, it becomes ready to be paid.

○ *The face amount of the policy is normally the amount paid when the policy matures.*

○ *The cash value, which may be less than the total sum of premiums paid, is paid to the policyholder when the contract matures or is surrendered.*

---

ma|ture² /mətʃʊər/

LIFE INSURANCE

ADJECTIVE A **mature** bond or life insurance policy is ready to be paid.

○ *The insurance remains in force until the insurance policy becomes mature.*

○ *The surrender value is what you get back if you cash in a life policy before it becomes mature.*

---

ma|tur|i|ty /mətʃʊərɪti/

LIFE INSURANCE

NOUN **Maturity** is the moment when a financial arrangement such as a bond or an insurance policy becomes ready to be paid.

○ *An endowment policy is designed to provide a lump sum on maturity.*

○ *The proceeds are the net amount of money payable by the company at the death of an insured or at the maturity of a policy.*

ma|tur|i|ty val|ue /mətʃʊərɪti vælyu/ (**maturity values**)

LIFE INSURANCE

NOUN The **maturity value** of a life insurance policy is the amount of money that is paid out when it matures.

○ The maturity value of an insurance policy becomes payable when the contract finishes or matures.

○ The maturity value of an endowment contract is the proceeds payable on it at the end of the specified endowment period.

max|i|mum life|time ben|e|fit /mæksɪməm laɪftaɪm bɛnɪfɪt/ (**maximum lifetime benefits**)

MEDICAL INSURANCE

NOUN The **maximum lifetime benefit** of a health insurance plan is the maximum amount of money that it will pay out.

○ Premium costs would be lowered further by establishing a maximum lifetime benefit for these subsidized policies, after which all costs would be paid by the public program.

○ A typical long-term care policy pays a fixed daily amount and a maximum lifetime benefit.

Med|i|caid /mɛdɪkeɪd/

MEDICAL INSURANCE

NOUN **Medicaid** is a medical benefits program in the U.S. administered by states and subsidized by the federal government.

○ In the United States, Medicaid provides some of the benefits of long-term care insurance.

○ Medicaid provides public assistance to persons whose income and resources are insufficient to pay for health care.

med|i|cal pro|ce|dure /mɛdɪkəl prəsidʒər/ (**medical procedures**)

MEDICAL INSURANCE

NOUN A **medical procedure** is a medical treatment or operation.

○ The medical expense policy specifies that the amount paid for a claim must conform to the amount most frequently charged for a medical procedure in a given geographical area.

m

○ *In health care insurance, the allowable fee is the maximum amount an insurer will pay for a medical procedure.*

---

med|i|cal un|der|writ|ing /mɛdɪkəl ʌndərraɪtɪŋ/

MEDICAL INSURANCE

NOUN **Medical underwriting** is the use of medical or health status information in the evaluation of an applicant for life or health insurance.

○ *People with diabetes typically have to pay more for health insurance, but some insurance companies have more lenient medical underwriting standards than others.*

○ *A process of medical underwriting is involved in impaired life annuities, which improve the terms offered due to a medical diagnosis which is severe enough to reduce life expectancy.*

Med|i|care /mɛdɪkɛər/

MEDICAL INSURANCE

NOUN **Medicare** is the federal government plan in the U.S. for paying certain hospital and medical expenses for elderly persons qualifying under the plan.

○ *Medicare covers a small fraction of long-term care and it is limited to skilled nursing care.*

○ *Medicare pays hospitals a set fee for treating patients in a single category, no matter what the actual cost of care for the person.*

Med|i|gap pol|i|cy /mɛdɪɡæp pɒlɪsi/ (**Medigap policies**)

MEDICAL INSURANCE

NOUN A **Medigap policy** is a private extra health insurance plan in the U.S. that provides coverage for medical expenses that are not or only partially covered by Medicare.

○ *A Medigap policy fills the gaps left in your original Medicare plan coverage, including deductibles and non-covered services.*

○ *A Medigap policy is a private insurance product that supplements Medicare insurance benefits.*

Med|i|vac /mɛdɪvæk/ (short for **medical evacuation**)

MEDICAL INSURANCE

NOUN **Medivac** is a service that provides medical care to injured patients while they are being transported from the scene of an accident to a hospital. This word is created from "medical" and "evacuation."

○ Medivac insurance covers the costs of airlifting you from a remote area, in a medically equipped vehicle.

○ Medivac is the timely and efficient movement and en route care provided by medical personnel to the wounded.

men|tal im|pair|ment /mɛntᵊl ɪmpɛərmənt/ (**mental impairments**)

MEDICAL INSURANCE

NOUN A **mental impairment** is a condition in which a part of a person's mind is damaged or is not working properly.

○ The policy defines a mental impairment as a loss of mental capacity that requires you to have substantial supervision to maintain your safety and the safety of others.

○ A worker is entitled to a cash disability benefit award because of an inability to work caused by any physical or mental impairment.

mit|i|gate a risk /mɪtɪgeɪt ə rɪsk/ (**mitigates a risk, mitigated a risk, mitigating a risk**)

GENERAL

PHRASE If something or someone **mitigates a risk**, they make the effects of a loss or risk less unpleasant, harmful, or serious.

○ Risk audits of the premises look at fire safety, fire systems, electrical safety, and industrial safety, and suggest suitable solutions to mitigate the risks at economical cost.

○ Burglar alarms, home security patrols, deadbolt locks, key secured windows are all ways of mitigating risk in home insurance.

mor|al haz|ard /mɔrəl hæʒərd/ (**moral hazards**)

GENERAL

NOUN A **moral hazard** is a risk that an insurance company has that policyholders may not be honest.

○ *There is a moral hazard in that, by offering excessive benefits, an incentive to claim could be created.*

○ *A moral hazard exists when the applicant may either want an outright loss to occur or may have a tendency to be less than careful with property.*

---

mor|bid|i|ty ta|ble /mɔrbɪdɪti teɪbᵊl/ (**morbidity tables**)

[**LIFE INSURANCE**]

NOUN A **morbidity table** is a statistical table that shows the proportion of people that are expected to become sick or injured at each age.

○ *The company must calculate a constant premium over the total lifetime of the contract at the time the policy is issued and base the calculation on an actuarial morbidity table.*

○ *The morbidity table shows the expected incidence of sickness or injury within a group during a period of time.*

---

mor|tal|i|ty rate /mɔrtælɪti reɪt/ (**mortality rates**)

[**LIFE INSURANCE**]

NOUN A **mortality rate** is the number of deaths during a particular period of time among a particular type or group of people.

○ *Insurers base the premiums for life insurance in part on the mortality rate for a proposed insured's age group.*

○ *Life expectancy of persons who attain age 65 appears to have lengthened by three years in the past ten, in part because the mortality rate from cardiac disease has fallen by 50 percent in five years.*

---

mor|tal|i|ty ta|ble (also known as **life table**) /mɔrtælɪti teɪbᵊl/ (**mortality tables**)

[**LIFE INSURANCE**]

NOUN A **mortality table** is a statistical table that shows how long people of each age are expected to live and how frequent deaths are for a given age or occupation.

○ *Insurers use a mortality table to determine the average duration of the life remaining to a number of persons of a given age.*

○ *By listing the mortality experience of individuals by age, a mortality table permits an actuary to calculate, on average, how long a male or female of a given age group may be expected to live.*

mort|gage in|sur|ance /mɔːrgɪdʒ ɪnʃʊərəns/

COMMERCIAL INSURANCE

NOUN **Mortgage insurance** is insurance that covers a person with a mortgage, and is intended to pay off the balance due on a mortgage if the insured dies or becomes disabled.

○ *Family heads buy mortgage insurance for the specific purpose of paying off any mortgage balance outstanding at their death.*

○ *Private mortgage insurance protects the lender against the default of higher risk loans.*

▶ SYNONYM:
   mortgage redemption insurance

mu|tu|al /myuːtʃuəl/

GENERAL

ADJECTIVE If a savings and loan association or an insurance company has **mutual** status, it is owned by its customers.

○ *Mutual companies are owned by the policyholders, while stock holders own stock insurance companies.*

○ *A mutual insurance company has no formal stockholders or capital stock, and is owned by its policyholders.*

mu|tu|al aid so|ci|e|ty /myuːtʃuəl eɪd səsaɪɪti/ (**mutual aid societies**)

MEDICAL INSURANCE

NOUN A **mutual aid society** is an organization that provides benefits or other help to its members when they are affected by things such as death, sickness, disability, old age, or unemployment.

○ *The most common model of a mutual aid society is probably a system of voluntary insurance, usually for income maintenance or health care, which offers social protection in return for a basic contribution.*

○ *The mutual aid society paid a death benefit, disability benefits, or medical benefits, and provided its funds to its members as needed.*

mu|tu|al fund /myuːtʃuəl fʌnd/ (**mutual funds**)

GENERAL

NOUN A **mutual fund** is a financial arrangement managed by an investment company, in which you can buy shares in many different businesses.

○ *The fund manager has the responsibility of overseeing the allocation of the pool of money invested in a particular mutual fund.*

○ *A mutual fund is a combination of contributions of many investors whose money is used to buy stocks, bonds, commodities, and options.*

---

mu|tu|al in|sur|ance /myyʊtʃuəl ɪnʃʊərəns/

GENERAL

NOUN Mutual insurance is a system of insurance in which policyholders are company members.

○ *With mutual insurance arrangements, each member contributes a sum of money entitling them to insurance protection, and at the end of the year dividends are paid out if there is a surplus.*

○ *A mutual insurance company is an insurance company without stockholders, whose management is directed by a board elected by the policyholders.*

---

mu|tu|al in|sur|er /myyʊtʃuəl ɪnʃʊərər/ (**mutual insurers**)

GENERAL

NOUN A **mutual insurer** is an insurance company which is owned by its members or policyholders rather than by shareholders.

○ *If at the end of the fiscal year the mutual insurer declares a profit, the profit is shared amongst all the policyholders.*

○ *Participating policyholders of a mutual insurer receive all the profits and other benefits of ownership.*

M|V|A /ɛm vi eɪ/ (short for **motor vehicle accident,** BRIT **RTA (road traffic accident)**)

VEHICLE INSURANCE

ABBREVIATION An **MVA** happens when a vehicle hits a person, an object, or another vehicle, causing injury or damage.

○ *Extremity symptoms such as arm and hand pain, numbness, and tingling are common following MVAs.*

○ *Failure to receive appropriate treatment for MVAs is a major contributor to the development of upper arm and hand symptoms.*

Nn

N|A|I|C /ɛn eɪ aɪ siː/ (short for **National Association of Insurance Commissioners**)

GENERAL

ABBREVIATION The **NAIC** is an organization in the U.S. which regulates the insurance industry and protects the interests of insurance clients.

- The NAIC Medical/Lifestyle Questions and Underwriting Guidelines prohibit insurers from making inquiries into a person's sexual orientation.

- The NAIC is an association of state insurance commissioners whose purpose is to promote uniformity of insurance regulation, monitor insurance solvency, and develop model laws for passage by state legislatures.

---

nat|u|ral ca|tas|tro|phe /nætʃərəl kətæstrəfi/ (**natural catastrophes**)

COMMERCIAL INSURANCE

NOUN A **natural catastrophe** is an unexpected event, caused by nature, such as an earthquake or flood, in which there is a lot of suffering, damage, or death.

- The lessons learned from earthquakes and hurricanes provide important strategies to understand natural catastrophe risk exposures.

- The policy rider covers a company in case of loss of revenue due to forced shutdown because of a natural catastrophe such as an earthquake or a fire or flood.

> **RELATED WORDS**
>
> An accident or event that happens because of natural causes can also be called an **act of God**. **Force majeure** is similar, but also includes events caused by humans, such as war.

neg|li|gence /nɛglɪdʒəns/

NOUN If someone is guilty of **negligence**, they have not taken enough care or have failed to do something which they ought to have done.

○ *Some errors may not be compensated at all, depending on whether the error was the result of negligence.*

○ *Professional indemnity insurance provides indemnity to professional individuals or firms against claims for financial loss for negligence due to failure to exercise the required degree of care.*

neg|li|gent /nɛglɪdʒənt/

ADJECTIVE If you are **negligent**, you do not take enough care of something or someone that you are responsible for, or you fail to do something which you ought to do.

○ *The purpose of liability insurance is to cover property damage to a third party resulting from the negligent or intentional acts of an insured.*

○ *Firms that are proven negligent in causing a worker's injury can be held liable.*

new busi|ness /nu bɪznɪs/

NOUN **New business** is the number of new policies that are written by an insurance company in a particular period.

○ *Typically expenses and reinsurance arrangements change after an insurer ceases to write new business.*

○ *Acquisition costs are costs associated with the underwriting of new business, including commission paid to brokers and agents.*

new busi|ness prof|it mar|gin /nu bɪznɪs prɒfɪt mɑrdʒɪn/ (**new business profit margins**)

NOUN A **new business profit margin** is a system used by insurers to measure the cost of and profit from writing new policies.

○ *A company's new business profit margin is defined as the value of new business expressed as a percentage of the present value of future premiums.*

○ *The insurer is planning to standardize its products as much as possible to reduce product development costs and thus increase the new business profit margin.*

---

no-fault in|sur|ance /noʊ fɔlt ɪnʃʊərəns/

VEHICLE INSURANCE

NOUN **No-fault insurance** is a type of insurance in the U.S. which pays an accident victim for medical and hospital expenses regardless of who was at fault in the accident.

○ *Under no-fault insurance, a person's own insurance company pays for financial losses like medical expenses and lost wages due to an accident, regardless of who caused it.*

○ *Under no-fault insurance, the injured party is entitled to medical, rehabilitation, and lost wage benefits from his or her own insurance company, irrespective of who caused the accident.*

---

no-load /noʊ loʊd/

LIFE INSURANCE

ADJECTIVE **No-load** life insurance is insurance that is not commission-based.

○ *To avoid these big charges against your cash value in the early years, you can purchase your life insurance from a discount insurance broker or a broker who specializes in no-load life insurance.*

○ *No-load annuity contracts do not have any deferred surrender charges and do not pay the financial professional a commission.*

---

non|con|trib|u|to|ry /nɒnkəntrɪbyətɔri/

LIFE INSURANCE

ADJECTIVE **Noncontributory** insurance is insurance that is completely paid for by the company, not the employee.

○ *The noncontributory employer-pay-all plan is simple, and it gives the employer full control over the plan.*

○ *Under a noncontributory employee benefit plan, the employer bears the full cost of the employees' benefits, and must insure all eligible employees.*

> **WORD BUILDER**
> **non-** = not
>
> The prefix **non-** often appears in words connected with not being
> or not doing something: **noncontributory**, **non-disclosure**,
> **nonparticipating**, **nonproportional**.

---

non-dis|clo|sure /nɒn dɪskloʊʒər/

UNDERWRITING

NOUN **Non-disclosure** is failure to inform an underwriter or insurer of all
the facts relating to a life or health insurance proposal.

  ○ A breach by way of omission could be committed either through non-
    disclosure of any material fact or by way of concealment of a material fact.

  ○ The policy shall become void at the option of the insurer in the event of any
    untrue or incorrect statement or non-disclosure in the proposal form.

---

non|par|tic|i|pat|ing /nɒnpərtɪsɪpeɪtɪŋ/

LIFE INSURANCE

ADJECTIVE A **nonparticipating** insurance policy does not give the right
to the policyholder to share in a company's profit.

  ○ With nonparticipating policies, the insurer does not distribute any part of
    surplus funds to policyholders.

  ○ Stock companies, in general, issue nonparticipating insurance, under which
    the insured is not entitled to share in the divisible surplus of the company.

---

non|pro|por|tion|al cov|er /nɒnprəpɔrʃənəl kʌvər/

REINSURANCE

NOUN **Nonproportional cover** is reinsurance cover such as excess of
loss reinsurance where the reinsurer's liability is not calculated as a
proportion of the insurance.

  ○ The coverage we place for our clients takes the form of a traditional structural
    mix of proportional reinsurance with nonproportional cover on the net
    retention.

  ○ With nonproportional cover, the reinsurer is liable only for losses which exceed
    the insurer's retention level, and premiums vary with loss expectation.

Oo

oc|cu|pa|tion /ɒkyəpeɪʃⁿn/ (occupations)

UNDERWRITING

NOUN A policyholder's **occupation** is their job or profession.

○ A disability is a physical or mental impairment that makes a person incapable of performing one or more duties of his or her occupation.

○ The insured will be considered disabled only if he or she is unable to work in an occupation for which he or she is qualified by education, training, or experience.

oc|cu|pa|tion|al group /ɒkyəpeɪʃənᵊl grup/ (occupational groups)

UNDERWRITING

NOUN An **occupational group** is a category used by insurance companies to classify jobs according to how hazardous they are.

○ The occupational group most at risk of violence at work is the group that contains police and prison officers.

○ Knowing a person's occupational group gives us insight into what this person's day might be like, and what risks they commonly face at work.

oc|cu|pa|tion|al haz|ard /ɒkyəpeɪʃənᵊl hæzərd/ (occupational hazards)

UNDERWRITING

NOUN An **occupational hazard** is a risk or danger that is connected to the job of the policyholder.

○ The premium for group insurance is calculated based on the characteristics of the group as a whole, such as average age and degree of occupational hazard.

○ Occupational hazards are conditions surrounding a work environment that increase the probability of death, disability, or illness to a worker.

o|cean ma|rine in|sur|ance /ˈoʊʃən məˈriːn ɪnˈʃʊərəns/

COMMERCIAL INSURANCE: MARINE INSURANCE

NOUN **Ocean marine insurance** is insurance for ships traveling by sea, including liabilities connected with them, and their cargoes.

○ Hull insurance is a class of ocean marine insurance that covers physical damage to the ship or vessel insured.

○ An ocean-going vessel intentionally sunk by its owner will not be covered by ocean marine insurance.

on-the-job in|ju|ry /ˌɒn ðə ˈdʒɒb ˈɪndʒəri/ (**on-the-job injuries**)

MEDICAL INSURANCE

NOUN **On-the-job injury** is bodily harm that is caused while you are doing your job.

○ In the event of the worker's death as the result of an on-the-job injury, the policy pays benefits to the worker's surviving dependents.

○ The injured employee will receive fast, reliable payment of lost wages and medical bills when an on-the-job injury occurs.

o|pen pol|i|cy /ˈoʊpən ˈpɒlɪsi/ (**open policies**)

COMMERCIAL INSURANCE

NOUN In marine insurance, an **open policy** is insurance for particular goods in which claims are settled on an ongoing basis after the loss or damage has occurred.

○ Whether cargoes are insured for a particular voyage or under open policies depends upon the volume and regularity with which a shipper uses ocean transit.

○ The basic use of an open policy is to enable the owner of goods to make a number of shipments and by declaring each shipment, to receive cover.

op|er|a|tion /ˌɒpəˈreɪʃ°n/ (**operations**)

MEDICAL INSURANCE

NOUN An **operation** is the process of cutting open someone's body in order to repair, replace, or remove a damaged part.

○ Surgical expense insurance covers the surgeon's charge for given operations or medical treatment.

○ *Before health insurance was common, people who needed an operation but couldn't afford it either died or suffered painful and disabling conditions.*

---

out|pa|tient /aʊtpeɪʃ°nt/ (**outpatients**)

MEDICAL INSURANCE

NOUN An **outpatient** is someone who goes to a hospital for treatment but does not stay overnight.

○ *Hospital benefits include reimbursement for both inpatient and outpatient medical care expenses.*

○ *Medical services that are provided on an outpatient or non-hospitalized basis may include diagnosis, treatment, and rehabilitation.*

---

o|ver|in|sured /oʊvərɪnʃʊərd/

GENERAL

ADJECTIVE If you are **overinsured**, you have too much insurance or the amount of your insurance is higher than the value of the items insured.

○ *As most of the risks don't apply to you, you are overinsured, and certainly do not need more coverage.*

○ *The life assured will be asked to disclose all other disability cover at new business stage so that the life office can ensure that he is not overinsured.*

> **RELATED WORDS**
>
> The opposite of **overinsured** is **underinsured**, when someone does not have enough insurance.

---

own oc|cu|pa|tion cov|er|age /oʊn ɒkyəpeɪʃ°n kʌvərɪdʒ/

MEDICAL INSURANCE

NOUN **Own occupation coverage** is insurance that covers a person if they cannot work in their own occupation, following an accident, injury, or disability.

○ *Own occupation coverage pays out if you become disabled and unable to do your job, even if you can earn more money doing another job.*

○ *Own occupation coverage allows policyholders to collect benefits if they are unable to perform all of the substantial and material duties of their own occupation.*

own or sim|i|lar oc|cu|pa|tion /oʊn ɔr sɪmɪlər ɒkyəpeɪʃən/

[MEDICAL INSURANCE]

PHRASE A policyholder's **own or similar occupation** is the job that they were doing before they became disabled or a job with similar duties and training.

○ *Own or similar occupation insurance pays out if the claimant is unable to perform their current profession or trade or a reasonable alternative based on their experience and qualifications.*

○ *If you are unable to engage in your own or similar occupation, you cannot perform the main functions of the job you held when you became disabled or of any similar job appropriate to your education, training, or experience.*

Pp

paid-up /peɪd ʌp/

LIFE INSURANCE

ADJECTIVE A **paid-up** insurance policy is one for which the payment of premiums has stopped.

○ A fully paid-up policy is one remaining in force after payment of all the premiums due under the terms of the policy.

○ A nonforfeiture option contained in most life insurance policies allows the insured to elect to have the cash surrender value of the policy used to purchase a paid-up policy for a reduced amount of insurance.

par|tial /pɑːʃ°l/

UNDERWRITING

ADJECTIVE A **partial** loss is a situation in which property covered by insurance is damaged but not completely destroyed, so that the insurer does not have to pay the full amount.

○ A partial loss under an insurance policy does not completely destroy or render worthless the insured property.

○ A partial loss is a loss involving less than all of the values insured or calling on the policy to pay less than its maximum amounts.

par|tic|i|pat|ing /pɑːtɪsɪpeɪtɪŋ/

LIFE INSURANCE

ADJECTIVE A **participating** health care provider is a doctor or hospital that has been approved by an insurer, so that if a policyholder uses their medical services, they will receive a discount.

○ The health insurance plan entitles members to services of participating physicians, hospitals, and clinics.

○ Medical care is provided to members of the health-care plan through a network of participating health-care providers.

par|tic|i|pat|ing in|sur|ance /pɑrtɪsɪpeɪtɪŋ ɪnʃʊərəns/

LIFE INSURANCE

NOUN **Participating insurance** is a system of insurance in which policyholders receive dividends from the company's profit.

○ Dividends are distributable to policyholders of participating insurance contracts as determined by the insurer and apportioned to policyholders on an equitable basis.

○ Dividends return part of the premium on participating insurance to policyholders to reflect the difference between the premium charged and the combination of actual mortality, expense, and investment experience.

> **RELATED WORDS**
>
> The opposite of this is **nonparticipating**, where policyholders do not have a right to a share in a company's profits.

par|tic|u|lar av|er|age /pərtɪkyələr ævərɪdʒ/

UNDERWRITING

NOUN **Particular average** is partial loss or damage to a ship or its cargo that affects only the ship owner or one cargo owner.

○ Particular average losses are those borne by the owners of the ship or cargo due to direct damage to their property.

○ Particular average is a partial loss that falls on one interest because it is not due to the type of situation to which the law of general average applies.

pay a claim /peɪ ə kleɪm/ (**pays a claim, paid a claim, paying a claim**)

CLAIMS

PHRASE If an insurer **pays a claim**, it pays money to a policyholder because a loss or risk occurs against which they were insured.

○ Insurers that paid claims on cargoes lost at sea now have the right to recover sunken treasures.

○ Insurance companies earn investment profits, because they have the use of the premium money from the time they receive it until the time they need it to pay claims.

pay a pen|sion /peɪ ə pɛnʃ°n/ (**pays a pension, paid a pension, paying a pension**)

LIFE INSURANCE: PENSIONS

PHRASE If a company or government **pays a pension** to someone, it provides them with money because they have reached a certain age.

○ *Many government retirement schemes are financed by payroll taxes so that the contributions made by today's workers are used to pay the pensions of those who have already retired.*

○ *The factory owners were unwilling to pay pensions to laid-off workers, many of whom had worked for the company for more than 20 years.*

pay|out /peɪaʊt/ (**payouts**)

CLAIMS

NOUN A **payout** is a sum of money paid to a policyholder when a claim is accepted.

○ *With many life insurance policies the only benefit received is a lump sum payout on death.*

○ *An immediate annuity begins regularly scheduled payouts within one year of purchase.*

> **TALKING ABOUT PAYOUTS**
>
> If a company puts a limit on the amount paid to a policyholder, it **caps** payouts. If it promises that policyholders will receive a certain amount, it **guarantees** payouts.

pay out /peɪ aʊt/ (**pays out, paid out, paying out**)

CLAIMS

VERB If an insurer **pays out**, it provides money to a policyholder because they have made a claim that has been accepted.

○ *You can easily add riders to a policy to create new conditions under which your insurance will or will not pay out.*

○ *In offering policies, insurance companies promise to pay out funds, up to the policy limits, under certain conditions for any covered accidents.*

P

per|il /pɛrɪl/ (perils)

UNDERWRITING

NOUN A **peril** is a great danger, especially of being harmed or killed.

○ *The extent of the perils covered depends on the type of policy.*

○ *Property insurance covers an insured's property against damage, destruction, or loss by an insured peril.*

per|son|al in|ju|ry /pɜrsənəl ɪndʒəri/ (personal injuries)

GENERAL

NOUN **Personal injury** is physical harm that is done to or suffered by someone.

○ *There is liability coverage should someone injure themselves while on your premises, need medical attention, and sue you for personal injury.*

○ *Robbery is the taking of property from a person by the threat of personal injury to that person.*

per|son|al in|ju|ry in|sur|ance /pɜrsənəl ɪndʒəri ɪnʃʊərəns/

GENERAL

NOUN **Personal injury insurance** is coverage for treatment of injuries to car accident victims, including loss of work income, accidental death, and funeral expenses.

○ *The government introduced a law that required every person who used a vehicle on the road to have at least third party personal injury insurance.*

○ *The personal injury insurance plan pays out of pocket expenses relating to bodily injuries.*

per|son|al li|a|bil|i|ty in|sur|ance /pɜrsənəl laɪəbɪlɪti ɪnʃʊərəns/

GENERAL

NOUN **Personal liability insurance** protects the insured if they are sued for claims that are covered by the insurance policy.

○ *Doctors, surgeons, nurses, and most other medical professionals are sometimes required to purchase personal liability insurance before becoming employed by a facility or opening a private practice.*

○ *The policy also provides a minimum of $100,000 of personal liability insurance that covers the tenant and spouse if either is sued because of property damage or bodily injury to another person.*

---

phys|i|cal im|pair|ment /fɪzɪkəl ɪmpɛərmənt/
(physical impairments)

MEDICAL INSURANCE

NOUN A **physical impairment** is a condition in which a part of a person's body is damaged or is not working properly.

○ *If your accident results in permanent physical impairment, you can sue the at-fault party to recover damages above and beyond your coverage.*

○ *Physical impairment is typically defined as not being able to perform without assistance two, or sometimes three, of the six basic activities of daily living.*

---

phy|si|cian /fɪzɪʃᵊn/ **(physicians)**

MEDICAL INSURANCE

NOUN A **physician** is a medical doctor.

○ *A physician is appointed by the medical director of a life or health insurer to examine applicants.*

○ *Any employee who leaves work because of a health condition, as certified by a physician, will be disqualified for benefits for a period of one to six weeks.*

---

plan /plæn/ **(plans)**

GENERAL

NOUN A **plan** is an insurance policy or contract, especially a life or health insurance policy.

○ *A life insurance plan is a major step you can take in order to assure the prosperity of your family.*

○ *Some plans allow withdrawal of accumulated growth at any time without penalties.*

---

plate glass in|sur|ance /pleɪt glæs ɪnʃʊərəns/

COMMERCIAL INSURANCE

NOUN **Plate glass insurance** is insurance coverage against damage to or breakage of large panes of glass such as shop windows.

○ *The plate-glass insurance covers accidental breakage of glass while situated at the insured's premises from any cause other than those specifically excluded in the policy.*

○ *Plate glass insurance covers loss of or damage to fixed plate glass by accidental means.*

P|M|I¹ /piː em aɪ/ (short for **private mortgage insurance**)

GENERAL

ABBREVIATION **PMI** is insurance provided by private mortgage insurers to protect lenders against loss if a borrower cannot pay repayments.

○ *PMI insures the lender in case the buyer defaults on the loan.*

○ *PMI is insurance written by a private company protecting the mortgage lender against loss occasioned by a mortgage default.*

P|M|I² /piː em aɪ/ (short for **private medical insurance**)

MEDICAL INSURANCE

ABBREVIATION **PMI** is insurance that pays for private medical expenses if the insured becomes sick or injured.

○ *PMI pays for the private treatment of short-term, curable illnesses known as acute conditions.*

○ *PMI plans discriminate in the kind of medical coverage they provide for certain illnesses of the brain.*

---

pol|i|cy /pɒlɪsi/ (**policies**)

GENERAL

NOUN A **policy** is an agreement that you have made with an insurance company, or a document that shows this.

○ *The policy will pay a specified sum to beneficiaries upon the death of the insured.*

○ *With a one-year insurance policy, half of the total premium has been earned after six months.*

TALKING ABOUT POLICIES

When you start a policy, you **open** it or **take** it **out**. When you end it, you **cancel** it.

When a policy is at the end of its period and there is money from it, it **matures**.

The things that are **covered** by a policy are those for which the policy will pay.

---

pol|i|cy|hold|er /pɒlısihoʊldər/ (**policyholders**)

GENERAL

NOUN A **policyholder** is a person who has an insurance policy with an insurance company.

○ *This provision in the policy reimburses the policyholder for the extra cost of living elsewhere while the house is being restored after a disaster.*

○ *A flood insurance policyholder should immediately report any flood loss to the insurance agent who wrote the policy.*

---

pol|i|cy is|su|ance /pɒlısi ınʃʊərəns/

GENERAL

NOUN **Policy issuance** is the process of creating an insurance policy and providing it to the policyholder.

○ *The policy owner must be permitted to convert to traditional whole life insurance within 24 months of policy issuance.*

○ *Coverage was barred for failure to disclose the risks of lead paint at the time of policy issuance.*

---

pol|i|cy loan /pɒlısi loʊn/ (**policy loans**)

LIFE INSURANCE

NOUN A **policy loan** is money that is borrowed against future benefits payable under a life insurance policy.

○ *You may borrow against a policy's cash value by taking out a policy loan.*

○ *The policyholder can use the cash value while continuing the insurance protection of the policy by taking a policy loan.*

---

pol|i|cy term /pɒlısi tɜrm/ (**policy terms**)

GENERAL

NOUN The **policy term** is the lifetime of an insurance policy.

○ *The policy will also pay out if death occurs before the end of the agreed policy term.*

○ *This policy will expire at 12:01 a.m. on the last day of the policy term.*

---

pol|i|cy word|ing /pɒlɪsi wɜrdɪŋ/

GENERAL

NOUN **Policy wording** is the terms and conditions and definitions of insurance coverage as they are written down in the insurance policy.

○ *Any ambiguity in an insurer's proposal form or policy wording will be construed against the insurer.*

○ *In order to avoid any dispute over risks covered, policy wording needs to be precise and clear.*

---

pool a risk /pul ə rɪsk/ (pools a risk, pooled a risk, pooling a risk)

REINSURANCE

PHRASE If an insurer **pools a risk**, it takes on a share of each risk underwritten by every other member in an association of insurers or reinsurers.

○ *Pooling risk is an important way insurers reduce the costs of bearing risk.*

○ *The savings provided by pooling risks allow insurance companies, even with overhead and expenses, to provide certain products and services more efficiently than one can duplicate on its own.*

---

port|a|bil|i|ty /pɔrtəbɪlɪti/

GENERAL

NOUN **Portability** is the ability of an employee to keep benefits, such as a pension plan or insurance coverage, when they change employers.

○ *Employer-based systems also reduce the portability of health insurance between jobs.*

○ *Portability allows for the transfer of pension rights and credits when a worker changes jobs.*

port|fo|li|o¹ /pɔrtfouliou/ (**portfolios**)

General

NOUN An insurer or reinsurer's **portfolio** is their total business.

○ There are concerns that some companies will face financial difficulties if their portfolio of business has an excessively high loss ratio.

○ While pensions must be priced according to their expected risk, smaller pensions must also be priced in relation to the additional uncertainty they cause in the portfolio overall.

port|fo|li|o² /pɔrtfouliou/ (**portfolios**)

General

NOUN A **portfolio** is one part of the business of an insurer or a reinsurer, such as the fire portfolio.

○ The company has continued to sustain profitable underwriting performance through management's initiatives in expense control in the major motor portfolio.

○ The fire portfolio remains the most profitable for most insurance companies, with a highly favorable claim experience of around 45 percent.

pos|ses|sions /pəzɛʃᵊnz/

Residence insurance

NOUN **Possessions** are all the items that a policyholder owns or has at a particular time and that are covered by a residential insurance policy.

○ Your estate is the total value of your possessions in whatever form they take.

○ The typical homeowners' insurance policy covers personal possessions inside the house such as furniture, appliances, and clothing, against a wide variety of perils.

P|P|A|C|A /pi pi eɪ si eɪ/ (short for **Patient Protection and Affordable Care Act**)

Medical insurance

ABBREVIATION The **PPACA** is a 2010 federal law that reformed some public health insurance programs and parts of the private health insurance industry in the U.S.

○ Under the PPACA, enacted in March 2010, small employers may be eligible to claim a tax credit of 35 percent of qualified health insurance premium costs paid by a taxable employer.

○ Many people believe that the PPACA, as a standalone health-insurance only reform, will not solve the problems of a very broken healthcare system.

---

pre|ex|ist|ing con|di|tion /priːgsɪstɪŋ kəndɪʃᵊn/ (**preexisting conditions**)

MEDICAL INSURANCE

NOUN A **preexisting condition** is a medical condition already suffered by a proposer before the starting date of an insurance policy.

○ Having a preexisting condition when shopping for health insurance can make the task a difficult one.

○ A preexisting condition was defined as one for which medical treatment or advice was rendered, prescribed, or recommended within 12 months prior to the participant's effective date of insurance.

---

pref|erred pro|vid|er or|gan|i|za|tion (ABBR PPO) /prɪfɜːrd prəvaɪdər ɔrgənəzeɪʃᵊn/ (**preferred provider organizations**)

MEDICAL INSURANCE

NOUN A **preferred provider organization** is an organization of hospitals and physicians who provide services to clients of a particular insurance company.

○ Providers in a preferred provider organization are under contract to an insurance company or health plan to provide care at a discounted or negotiated rate.

○ Preferred provider organizations are doctors and hospitals that agree to provide health care services to members of a particular group at fees negotiated in advance.

---

pref|erred pro|vid|er plan (ABBR PPP) /prɪfɜːrd prəvaɪdər plæn/ (**preferred provider plans**)

MEDICAL INSURANCE

NOUN A **preferred provider plan** is a health insurance plan in the U.S. written by an organization of hospitals and physicians who provide services to clients of a particular insurance company.

- Under a preferred provider plan, providers are under contract to an insurance company or health plan to provide care at a discounted or negotiated rate.
- With a preferred provider plan, you can choose from any doctor who is a member of the network for your medical care and switch doctors whenever you like.

---

pre|mi|um /ˈpriːmiəm/ (premiums)

GENERAL

NOUN   A **premium** is the cost of insurance, that is usually an amount paid each year.

- An annuity was purchased by the payment of annual premiums for a specified period of time.
- If the premium we received from you was not enough to buy the kind and amount of coverage you requested, we will provide only the amount of coverage that can be purchased for the payment we received.

> **TALKING ABOUT PREMIUMS**
>
> Insurance companies **charge** premiums and customers **pay** them. When companies **calculate** their premiums, they decide how much they will cost.
>
> Customers usually pay **monthly** or **annual** premiums.
>
> If a company decides that a customer does not have to pay a premium, they **waive** that premium.

---

pre|mi|um in|come /ˈpriːmiəm ˈɪnkʌm/

GENERAL

NOUN   An insurer's **premium income** is the income that it earns from premiums.

- The insurance company's annual premium income exceeds $15 million from over two dozen products.
- To an insurer, the risk is that people live longer than expected, requiring a greater number of payouts for the same initial amount of premium income.

pri|ma|ry in|sur|er /praɪməri ɪnʃʊərər/ (primary insurers)

REINSURANCE

NOUN A **primary insurer** is the insurance company that first sells insurance to a client, who later purchases reinsurance.

○ To protect the insurance company from major losses, the primary insurer will typically hold a designated amount of the risk themselves, and amounts in excess of that are placed with a reinsurance company.

○ The primary insurer is the ceding company that initially originates the business.

▶ SYNONYM:
ceding company

pri|vate health in|sur|ance /praɪvɪt hɛlθ ɪnʃʊərəns/

MEDICAL INSURANCE

NOUN **Private health insurance** is insurance taken out in case you need to have medical treatment as a private patient.

○ Currently 85 percent of the population is covered by a basic statutory health insurance plan, and the remainder opt for private health insurance, which frequently offers additional benefits.

○ Today, most comprehensive private health insurance programs cover the cost of routine, preventive, and emergency health care procedures.

TYPES OF HEALTH INSURANCE

The following are all types of insurance that people take out to protect them in the event of illness.

any occupation insurance, critical illness insurance, dental insurance, disability insurance, income protection insurance, own occupation coverage

---

prob|a|ble max|i|mum loss /prɒbəbəl mæksɪməm lɔs/ (probable maximum losses)

REINSURANCE

NOUN **Probable maximum loss** is the maximum amount of loss that can be expected under normal circumstances.

○With $1 million at risk but a probable maximum loss of $100,000, for example, the property owner would probably buy $100,000 insurance and bank on avoiding the larger disaster.

○The probable maximum loss is the largest loss thought probable under an insurance policy; normally applied to material damage risks where the total sum insured is not considered to be at risk from one loss event.

---

prod|uct li|a|bil|i|ty in|sur|ance (ABBR **PLI**) /prɒdʌkt laɪəbɪlɪti ɪnʃʊərəns/

COMMERCIAL INSURANCE

NOUN Product liability insurance is insurance for a producer or supplier of goods against injury to third parties or loss of or damage to their property that is caused by a fault in the goods.

○A product manufacturer may purchase product liability insurance to cover them if a product is faulty and causes damage to the purchasers or any other third party.

○The legislation requires those manufacturing or supplying goods to carry some form of product liability insurance, usually as part of a combined liability policy.

---

pro|fes|sion|al li|a|bil|i|ty in|sur|ance (ABBR **PLI**) /prəfɛʃənªl laɪəbɪlɪti ɪnʃʊərəns/

COMMERCIAL INSURANCE

NOUN Professional liability insurance is insurance for a company or a professional person against claims or financial losses that may occur as a result of their negligence.

○Many small businesses do not secure professional liability insurance due to the high cost of premiums.

○Typically, professional liability insurance protects technology firms from litigation resulting from charges of professional negligence or failure to perform professional duties.

---

prom|is|so|ry /prɒmɪsɔri/

GENERAL

ADJECTIVE A promissory note or warranty states how the provisions of an insurance contract will be fulfilled after it has been signed.

○ *The promissory warranty includes undertakings by the insured that something be done or omitted after the policy takes effect and during its continuance.*

○ *A promissory warranty describes a condition, fact, or circumstance to which the insured agrees to be held during the life of the contract.*

---

proof of cov|er|age /pruf əv kʌvərɪdʒ/ (proofs of coverage)

GENERAL

NOUN A policyholder's **proof of coverage** is a document from an insurer stating that they have insurance coverage.

○ *Some states with compulsory insurance require proof of coverage when a vehicle is registered and when a driver is stopped for a traffic violation.*

○ *Drivers are asked to show proof of coverage when involved in an accident, stopped by the police, or when they renew their driver's license.*

---

prop|er|ty /prɒpərti/

RESIDENCE INSURANCE

NOUN A policyholder's **property** is the thing or things that they own.

○ *The liability portion of the policy covers the homeowner for accidental injuries caused to third parties or their property.*

○ *The personal property that is moved to protect it from flood must be placed in a fully enclosed building or otherwise reasonably protected from the elements.*

---

prop|er|ty and cas|u|al|ty in|sur|ance /prɒpərti ənd kæʒuəlti ɪnʃuərəns/

GENERAL

NOUN **Property and casualty insurance** is insurance on homes, cars, and businesses, rather than health or life insurance.

○ *Basically there is a broad insurance distinction between companies writing life and health insurance and those writing property and casualty insurance.*

○ *Property and casualty insurance agents and brokers sell policies that protect individuals and businesses from financial loss as a result of risks such as automobile accidents, fire or theft, and tornadoes and storms.*

pro|por|tion|al re|in|sur|ance cov|er|age
/prəpɔːʃənᵊl riːɪnʃʊərəns kʌvərɪdʒ/

REINSURANCE

NOUN **Proportional reinsurance coverage** is reinsurance of part of original insurance premiums and losses being shared between a reinsurer and insurer.

○ With proportional reinsurance coverage, the ceding company and the reinsurer share risks and premiums on a proportional basis.

○ Under proportional reinsurance coverage, the insurer and the reinsurer both share the premiums and the claims on a given risk in a specified proportion.

pro|po|sal /prəpəʊzəl/ (proposals)

SALES AND DISTRIBUTION

NOUN A **proposal** is a request for insurance coverage submitted by a prospective client to an insurer.

○ The proposal usually includes sufficient facts for the insurer to determine whether or not he wishes to accept the risk.

○ A contract of marine insurance is concluded between the parties when the proposal is accepted by the insurer.

pro|po|sal form /prəpəʊzəl fɔːm/ (proposal forms)

SALES AND DISTRIBUTION

NOUN A **proposal form** is a standard printed document that is completed by a person who is requesting insurance coverage.

○ The main source of information in an application for risk coverage is the proposal form that the applicant or the intermediary submits to the insurer.

○ A duly completed proposal form is the basis of insurance, and any changes at each renewal may be advised by the insured to the insurer by a letter signed by the insured.

pro|pos|er /prəpəʊzər/ (proposers)

SALES AND DISTRIBUTION

NOUN A **proposer** is a person who submits a request for insurance coverage.

○ *The proposer of an insurance request must disclose all material facts which would influence a prudent insurer in deciding whether to accept the insurance and if so on what terms.*

○ *The proposer becomes the insured when the application has been accepted and the contract brought into being.*

---

pro|vi|sion¹ /prəvɪʒᵊn/

LIFE INSURANCE

NOUN If you **make provision** for yourself or your family, you ensure that you or they will have sufficient income in the future, especially during retirement.

○ *Personal pensions are designed to allow anyone who is not a member of an occupational pension scheme to make provision for a pension in retirement.*

○ *A last survivor death benefit is ideal to make provision for the needs of the children in the event of the simultaneous death of the two parents.*

---

pro|vi|sion² /prəvɪʒᵊn/ (**provisions**)

GENERAL

NOUN A **provision** is a condition in an insurance contract or agreement.

○ *A premium refund is a special provision in the policy which allows a beneficiary to collect the face amount of a policy plus all the premiums that have been paid.*

○ *A provision in the policy requires that the injury be accidental in order for benefits to be payable.*

Qq

quo|ta share re|in|sur|ance /kwˈoʊtə ʃeər riːɪnʃʊərəns/

NOUN **Quota share reinsurance** is a form of reinsurance in which the reinsurer accepts a certain percentage of all or certain parts of the business of the reinsured person or company.

○ Quota share reinsurance requires the insurer to transfer, and the reinsurer to accept, a given percentage of every risk within a defined category of business written by the insurer.

○ With quota share reinsurance, the reinsurer may be asked to assume a quota share of a gross account, paying its share of premium for other reinsurance protecting that gross account.

quote¹ /kwˈoʊt/ (quotes)

NOUN A **quote** is an estimate of the price of insurance coverage that is given to a proposer by an insurer or an intermediary before they decide which policy to choose.

○ Since there are plenty of policies and premium rates available, it helps to compare life insurance quotes.

○ To make accurate comparisons between car insurance quotes, you will need to make sure you are comparing policies with the same level of coverage and the same deductible.

quote² /kwˈoʊt/ (quotes, quoted, quoting)

VERB If an insurer **quotes** a price to a proposer, it gives them an estimate of the price of insurance coverage.

q

○ The competitiveness of the market for private mortgage insurance suggests that quoted prices are good approximations of the minimum cost of providing such insurance.

○ The cheapest premium quoted for life cover may be more expensive if you have any health issues.

Rr

real es|tate / riːl ɪsteɪt/

NOUN **Real estate** is property in the form of land, houses or other buildings.

○ *Title insurance guarantees the purchaser of real estate against loss from undiscovered defects in the title to property that has been purchased.*

○ *Personal property is property other than real estate, or property that is movable or separable from it.*

real es|tate in|sur|ance /riːl ɪsteɪt ɪnʃʊərəns/

NOUN **Real estate insurance** is insurance of property, land, and buildings.

○ *Real estate insurance provides coverage for property owners who lease or rent building space used for offices, service businesses, or retail stores.*

○ *Real estate insurance policies often include replacement insurance terms for reconstruction costs of repairing or rebuilding real estate that is subsequently damaged.*

re al es|tate li|a|bil|i|ty /riːl ɪsteɪt laɪəbɪlɪti/

NOUN **Real estate liability** is liability for risks that come from owning real estate.

○ *Real estate liability is legal liability connected with the use, sales, and trades of real estate.*

○ *Real estate liability assessments have become a necessary step for lenders, property owners, and prospective buyers to determine potential environmental liabilities associated with real estate transactions.*

re|bate /rɪ̱beɪt/ (rebates)

GENERAL

NOUN A **rebate** is an amount of money that is returned to you from an insurer's profits, or when you have paid too high premiums.

○ *A mutual insurance company has no stock, and any operating profit is paid to their insureds in the form of a premium rebate.*

○ *If your losses stay under certain thresholds after a predetermined period, you receive a premium rebate from the insurer's profit after the predetermined date.*

re|cov|er|y /rɪkʌ̱vəri/ (recoveries)

CLAIMS

NOUN A **recovery** is money received by an insurer to reduce part of the cost of a loss.

○ *Recoveries may be made from several different sources, such as reinsurers, other insurers, salvage, or liable third parties.*

○ *A net loss is the amount of loss sustained by an insurer after making deductions for all recoveries, salvage, and all claims upon reinsurers.*

re|duce a risk /rɪdu̱s ə rɪ̱sk/ (reduces a risk, reduced a risk, reducing a risk)

GENERAL

PHRASE If you **reduce a risk**, you lessen the potential damage that could be caused by a hazard or danger.

○ *There are several strategies safety professionals recommend to help reduce the risk of weather-related accidents.*

○ *The first step in risk management is to analyze exposures to risk and reduce the risk with safety measures.*

ref|use a pro|po|sal /rɪfyu̱z ə prəpo̱ʊzəl/ (refuses a proposal, refused a proposal, refusing a proposal)

UNDERWRITING

PHRASE If an insurer **refuses a proposal**, it does not agree to underwrite a risk proposed by a potential client.

○ *If one insurer refuses your proposal, this does not mean that others will also do the same, as different underwriters have different perceptions of risk.*

○ *The insurer reserves the right to refuse a proposal from motorists who have poor driving records.*

reg|u|lar pre|mi|um /rɛgyələr primiəm/ (regular premiums)

GENERAL

NOUN A **regular premium** is money paid to buy insurance coverage in installments at particular time intervals, such as monthly or annually.

○ *You may also choose to pay a single premium at the start of the policy, instead of having to arrange regular premium payments.*

○ *Traditional policies would require the policyholder to make regular premium payments and would provide for payment of a predetermined sum if the policyholder died during the specified term of the policy.*

re|im|burse /riɪmbɜrs/ (reimburses, reimbursed, reimbursing)

GENERAL

VERB If an insurer **reimburses** a policyholder, it pays them the expenses incurred as a loss covered by the insurance policy.

○ *A provision in the policy reimburses the policyholder for the extra cost of living elsewhere while the house is being restored after a disaster.*

○ *A health savings account can be used to pay for certain medical expenses not reimbursed by the benefit plan.*

WORD BUILDER

re- = again

The prefix **re-** often appears in words that relate to doing something again: **reimburse**, **reinsurance**, **renew**, **repatriate**, **replacement**.

---

re|im|burse|ment /riɪmbɜrsmənt/

GENERAL

NOUN **Reimbursement** is payment of the expenses incurred as a loss covered by an insurance policy.

○ *Pet insurance plans generally require customers to pay the vet bill first and then submit receipts for reimbursement.*

○ *The insurance provides reimbursement of the expenses actually incurred as a result of an accident or sickness that do not exceed any amount specified in the policy.*

re|in|sur|ance (BRIT reassurance) /riɪnʃʊərəns/

| REINSURANCE |

NOUN **Reinsurance** is insurance protection taken out by an insurer to limit its exposure to losses on an original insurance contract.

- ○ *A property insurer may not be able to buy reinsurance to protect its own bottom line unless it keeps its potential maximum losses under a certain level.*
- ○ *The purpose of reinsurance is for a company to avoid having too large a risk or concentration of risks, within the company.*

re|in|sur|ance trea|ty /riɪnʃʊərəns triti/ (reinsurance treaties)

| REINSURANCE |

NOUN A **reinsurance treaty** is a contract that defines the terms of reinsurance business.

- ○ *The reinsurer will be obliged to pay for losses that have occurred prior to commencement of the reinsurance treaty but unsettled at the end of the previous contract period.*
- ○ *The reinsurance treaty is negotiated and signed by a ceding company and a reinsurer and establishes the terms and conditions by which risk can be submitted for reinsurance.*

re|in|sure (BRIT reassure) /riɪnʃʊər/ (reinsures, reinsured, reinsuring)

| REINSURANCE |

VERB If an insurer **reinsures** a risk, they purchase reinsurance to cover it.

- ○ *Risks are evaluated on a case-by-case basis, allowing ceding insurers to reinsure dangerous risks which are not covered by continuing contract.*
- ○ *The amount of risk a company reinsures with a second company varies from carrier to carrier.*

re|in|sur|er /riɪnʃʊərər/ (reinsurers)

| REINSURANCE |

NOUN A **reinsurer** is an insurance company that insures the risks of other insurance companies.

- ○ *A cedant is an insurer who transfers all or part of a risk to a reinsurer.*
- ○ *The reinsurer covers all the insurance policies coming within the scope of the reinsurance contract.*

re|new /rɪnu̲/ (renews, renewed, renewing)

VERB If you **renew** an existing insurance contract, you continue it for a further period.

○ *Some insurance policyholders renew their insurance contract without having it reviewed annually.*

○ *The insurance company has the right to decline to renew the contract at the end of the policy term only under conditions defined in the contract.*

re|new|a|ble term in|sur|ance /rɪnu̲əbəl tɜrm ɪnʃʊərəns/

NOUN **Renewable term insurance** is term life insurance that may be renewed for another period without the policyholder needing to provide further evidence of their insurability.

○ *Premiums on ordinary annual renewable term insurance policies increase in cost every year.*

○ *Renewable term insurance can be renewed at the end of the term, at the option of the policyholder and without evidence of insurability, for a limited number of successive terms.*

re|new|al /rɪnu̲əl/

NOUN The **renewal** of an existing insurance contract is the act of continuing it for a further period.

○ *The rates of the policy increase at each renewal as the age of the insured increases.*

○ *The renewal of an insurance policy provides continuance of coverage beyond its original term by the insurer's acceptance of the premium for a new policy term.*

re|new|al date /rɪnu̲əl deɪt/ (renewal dates)

NOUN The **renewal date** of an existing insurance contract is the date on which it must be renewed.

○ *If your insurer intends to increase your premium by 10 percent or more upon renewal, the insurer must send you notice of the rate increase at least 30 days before your renewal date.*

○ *Upon the annual renewal date, an insurance company will often try to encourage you to upgrade to a new policy.*

---

rent|er /rɛntər/ (renters)

RESIDENCE INSURANCE

NOUN A **renter** is a person who is paying to live in a residence that does not belong to them.

○ *The rental agreements contractually obligate the renter to pay costs not covered by normal insurance.*

○ *If you are a renter, it is your landlord who needs protection against damage to the building itself, but you yourself need protection against damage to or theft of your personal property.*

---

rent|er's in|sur|ance /rɛntərz ɪnʃʊərəns/

RESIDENCE INSURANCE

NOUN Renter's insurance is insurance for renters to insure their property against loss.

○ *Also available is a renter's insurance, which provides personal property insurance for tenants.*

○ *Renter's insurance is very much like a homeowner's policy without the property coverage since renters do not own the building they live in.*

---

re|pat|ri|ate /ripeɪtrieɪt/ (repatriates, repatriated, repatriating)

MEDICAL INSURANCE

VERB If a claimant or their body is **repatriated**, they are transported back to their own country after they have been injured or killed in a foreign country.

○ *The parents of the dead man have discovered that they will have to pay the full cost of repatriating their son's body themselves because he did not have insurance.*

○ *Most travel insurance policies do pay to repatriate bodies or ashes if the policyholder has died abroad.*

re|pat|ri|a|tion /ripeitrieiʃᵊn/

RESIDENCE INSURANCE

MEDICAL INSURANCE

NOUN **Repatriation** is the process of transporting a claimant or their body back to their own country after they have been injured or killed in a foreign country.

○ *Some companies also offer other benefits, for example assistance with legal expenses and repatriation of the deceased's remains.*

○ *Some travel insurance will pay for repatriation of a person's remains to their home country if they die on a trip.*

re|pat|ri|a|tion ex|pens|es /ripeitrieiʃᵊn ikspɛnsiz/

MEDICAL INSURANCE

NOUN **Repatriation expenses** are the costs involved in transporting a claimant or their body back to their own country after they have been injured or killed in a foreign country.

○ *The policy covers hospitalization expenses, or repatriation expenses for transporting the mortal remains of the insured back to their native country.*

○ *Travel policies cover a wide range of possible claims which include overseas medical expenses and repatriation expenses, if a policyholder dies while on a trip.*

re|place|ment cost ba|sis /ripleismənt kɔst beisis/

RESIDENCE INSURANCE

NOUN **Replacement cost basis** is a method of valuing insured property in which the cost of replacing property is calculated without a reduction for depreciation.

○ *A provision allows settlement of losses to outbuildings to be on a replacement cost basis in lieu of actual cash value under the current policy.*

○ *Your building and contents will be written on a replacement cost basis which would replace items lost with payment equal to today's purchase price of those items, with no deduction for depreciation.*

re|place|ment cost in|sur|ance /ripleismənt kɔst inʃvərəns/

RESIDENCE INSURANCE

NOUN **Replacement cost insurance** is insurance in which the cost of replacing property is calculated without a reduction for depreciation.

○ *The older the building, the more important replacement cost insurance becomes.*

○ *Replacement cost insurance will pay the policy owner the full cost of replacing the lost or damaged property, subject to a maximum amount.*

---

re|port a claim /rɪpɔrt ə klɛɪm/ (reports a claim, reported a claim, reporting a claim)

GENERAL

PHRASE If you **report a claim**, you inform an insurer that an insured event has occurred and that you intend to ask the insurer for financial payment.

○ *Even if it seems like the injury is minor, report the claim to your insurer quickly.*

○ *If you cannot reach your insurance agent, report your claim directly by calling the claims department.*

---

re|port an ac|ci|dent /rɪpɔrt ən æksɪdənt/ (reports an accident, reported an accident, reporting an accident)

GENERAL

PHRASE If you **report an accident**, you inform an insurer or the police or other authorities that an accident has occurred.

○ *Not reporting an accident could be a breach of your insurance contract, leading to many unexpected consequences.*

○ *The judgment ruled that the claimant did not report the accident in time, and the insurance carrier was, therefore, relieved of liability for any benefits.*

---

re|scind a con|tract /rɪsɪnd ə kɒntrækt/ (rescinds a contract, rescinded a contract, rescinding a contract)

GENERAL

PHRASE If an insurer **rescinds an insurance contract**, it terminates it because facts have been concealed or misrepresented by the proposer.

○ *The fraudulent intent on the part of the insured must be established to entitle the insurer to rescind the insurance contract.*

○ *The insurer has the right to rescind the insurance contract for material misrepresentations and omissions in the policyholder's application.*

re|scis|sion /rɪsɪʃᵊn/

GENERAL

NOUN **Rescission** is the termination of an insurance contract by the insurer because facts have been concealed or misrepresented by the proposer.

○ *An insurer usually seeks a rescission of an insurance policy when there has been a material misrepresentation in the insurance application.*

○ *A breach of utmost good faith, especially in regard to full and voluntary disclosure of the elements of risk or loss, is accepted as grounds for rescission of the insurance contract.*

re|serves /rɪzɜrvz/

GENERAL

NOUN **Reserves** are funds that an insurer sets aside to pay future claims.

○ *Insurers often accumulate reserves to strengthen their financial structure.*

○ *To increase its capacity, an insurer will have to demonstrate that it has adequate reserves to meet any potential losses.*

TALKING ABOUT RESERVES

If something **depletes** an organization's reserves, it uses them and makes them lower. Reserves that are falling are often described as **dwindling**. Something that uses reserves is a **drain on** reserves.

If an organization replaces reserves that have been spent, it **replenishes** them, and if it gets more and more reserves, it **accumulates** them.

---

res|i|dence in|sur|ance /rɛzɪdəns ɪnʃʊərəns/

RESIDENCE INSURANCE

NOUN **Residence insurance** is insurance coverage against damage to a building in which you live.

○ *Residence insurance providers will demand that you have protection for at the very least 80 percent of the value of the home.*

○ *Residence insurance is an important part of home ownership.*

re|sid|u|al /rɪzɪdʒuəl/

GENERAL

ADJECTIVE **Residual** debt is money that remains to be paid and is still owed to someone.

○ *If necessary, the mortgage could be extended to cover any residual debt at the end of the year.*

○ *The scheme can also allow freezing or reduction of interest during a repayment program and the write-off of residual debt on successful completion of the program.*

re|sid|u|al debt in|sur|ance /rɪzɪdʒuəl dɛt ɪnʃʊərəns/

GENERAL

NOUN **Residual debt insurance** is a type of risk insurance that banks often require when granting a loan, which is used to guarantee that the loan is repaid in the event of death or disability.

○ *Residual debt insurance policies cover the borrower's risk of being unable to pay back the loan to the bank, for example, in case of unemployment or death.*

○ *A residual debt insurance policy is a special type of risk insurance which is used to guarantee that the loan is repaid in the event of death or disability.*

re|tain /rɪteɪn/ (retains, retained, retaining)

GENERAL

VERB If an insurer **retains** a risk, it keeps it rather than reinsuring.

○ *A starting insurance company has a low capacity to retain risks, and is thus forced to reinsure a large part of its business.*

○ *The primary insurer retained most of the accepted risks for its own account.*

re|ten|tion /rɪtɛnʃən/

CLAIMS

NOUN **Retention** of clients or money is the process of ensuring that a policyholder remains a customer of the insurer or that money to be paid out remains in the insurer's accounts.

○ *Increasing the insurance company's product range increases client loyalty and client retention.*

○ *Retention of business from existing brokers and clients is a key feature of our company's strategy.*

re|ten|tion of risk /rɪtɛnʃᵊn əv rɪsk/

Reinsurance

NOUN **Retention of risk** is the net amount of any risk which an insurance company does not reinsure but keeps for its own account.

○ The reinsurer will indemnify the ceding company against the amount of loss on each risk in excess of a specified retention of risk subject to a specified limit.

○ Often a maximum net retention of risk is specified in the treaty, with the primary company having the option to choose to retain less for its own account on individual risks.

re|tire /rɪtaɪər/ (retires, retired, retiring)

Life insurance: Pensions

VERB If you **retire**, you stop work when you have reached a certain age, usually when you are eligible for Social Security or a pension.

○ Since the annuity is received after you have retired from active employment, the effective rate of tax comes down drastically.

○ Coverage ends at age 70, and if you retire after age 70, coverage ends at retirement.

re|tir|ee /rɪtaɪəri/ (retirees)

Life insurance: Pensions

NOUN A **retiree** is a person who has retired.

○ Many retirees fail to consider inflation in their estimates of their retirement income.

○ Benefits will be based on wages, which are a measure of the income that retirees need to replace.

re|tire|ment /rɪtaɪərmənt/

Life insurance: Pensions

NOUN **Retirement** is the time when you stop working, usually because of your age, or the period when you have stopped working.

○ There are many plans that will help to ensure a regular income stream after retirement.

○ The study discovered that pension and other sources of retirement income were even less common for minorities and unmarried women.

> **WORD BUILDER**
> **-ment** = action or process
>
> The suffix **-ment** is often added to verbs to form nouns connected with actions or processes: **endorsement**, **endowment**, **impairment**, **payment**, **reimbursement**, **retirement**, **settlement**.

---

re|tire|ment age /rɪtaɪərmənt eɪdʒ/

LIFE INSURANCE: PENSIONS

NOUN **Retirement age** is the age at which people usually stop working, usually when they are eligible for Social Security or a pension.

○ *Although the retirement age has increased, it has not kept pace with the increase in life expectancies.*

○ *The government proposals would raise the minimum retirement age to 68 from 60 and 65 and base the amount of the pension on the career income average rather than final salary.*

---

ret|ro|ces|sion /rɛtrəsɛʃᵊn/

REINSURANCE

NOUN **Retrocession** is the reinsuring of a risk by a reinsurer.

○ *A retrocession is placed to afford additional capacity to the original reinsurer, or to contain or reduce the original reinsurer's risk of loss.*

○ *Reinsurance companies cede risks under retrocession agreements to other reinsurers, for reasons similar to those that cause primary insurers to purchase reinsurance.*

---

re|ver|sion /rɪvɜrʒᵊn/

LIFE INSURANCE

NOUN **Reversion** is a system by which a property owner sells part of their property to an insurance company while still having the right to live there.

○ *With a reversion plan, the home is sold to an insurance company that then pays a regular income to the owner.*

○ *Because the money from the home reversion scheme is provided upfront and you continue to live in your home rent free, you'll get less than the full market value of the share of the property that you sell.*

re|ver|sion|ar|y bo|nus /rɪvɜrʒᵊnɛri boʊnəs/ (**reversionary bonuses**)

NOUN A **reversionary bonus** is a bonus added to the value of a life insurance policy.

○ *The profits are allocated to each with-profit policy and are paid as reversionary bonuses in addition to the specified sum insured.*

○ *Holders of with-profits policies will receive a share in the surplus usually by allocation as a reversionary bonus added to the sum assured and payable with it.*

re|view|a|ble /rɪvyuəbᵊl/

ADJECTIVE **Reviewable** premiums or payments are not guaranteed and may be increased or decreased.

○ *Coverage which operates on a reviewable payment basis will have payments guaranteed for the first five years.*

○ *If you choose reviewable premiums, these are reviewed every five years and could increase or decrease.*

> **WORD BUILDER**
> **-ible/-able** = able to be done
>
> The suffix **-ible** or **-able** often appears in adjectives that mean that a particular thing can be done to something: **deductible**, **eligible**, **insurable**, **liable**, **reviewable**.

rid|er /raɪdər/ (**riders**)

NOUN A **rider** is an extra piece of information that is added to an insurance contract to change it by, for example, including a risk or an additional premium.

○ *Homeowners may buy earthquake insurance from an insurance company as an optional rider to a fire insurance policy.*

○ *Riders may be added to a policy to expand or limit the benefits otherwise payable.*

ri|ot /ˈraɪət/ (riots)

COMMERCIAL INSURANCE

NOUN When there is a **riot**, a crowd of people behave violently in a public place, fighting, and damaging buildings and vehicles.

○ Specific exclusions such as fraud, war, riot, and civil commotion, are often written into the contract to limit the liability of the insurer.

○ Coverage includes acts of striking employees at the insured location, and looting occurring at the time of the riot or civil commotion.

risk /rɪsk/ (risks)

GENERAL

NOUN A **risk** is a person or thing that is insured against as it may be harmed, damaged, or lost.

○ The policy wording needs to be precise, and certain risks may be excluded from the coverage in order to keep the premium affordable.

○ In individual insurance, each person's risk potential is evaluated to determine insurability.

risk ex|cess of loss /rɪsk ˈɛksɛs əv lɔs/

REINSURANCE

NOUN **Risk excess of loss** is a type of reinsurance that is given to an insurer to protect against a single loss or risk incurred at a specified amount.

○ Under risk excess of loss reinsurance, the insurer remains liable only for risks up to a maximum amount per claim, which enables an insurer to underwrite risks that it could not otherwise manage.

○ Risk excess of loss insurance is used when the primary insurer wants to limit his loss per risk or policy.

risk man|age|ment /rɪsk ˈmænɪdʒmənt/

GENERAL

NOUN **Risk management** is a system of preventing or reducing the likelihood that dangerous accidents or mistakes will occur, or reducing the amount of money lost by the insurance company.

○ Operational risk management involves structuring the organization so that when something bad does happen, the company can absorb that hit in the best way possible.

○ *An employer needs to be aware of the claims an employee can bring, risk management techniques to avoid or lessen the potentiality of a claim, and the insurance available to cover those claims.*

---

risk man|ag|er /rɪsk mænɪdʒər/ (**risk managers**)

GENERAL

NOUN A **risk manager** is a person who works in risk management.

○ *Exclusions in the policy are important, and should be reviewed with a qualified risk manager.*

○ *Computerized data permits the risk manager to analyze risk and to use this information to predict future loss levels.*

---

risk pool|ing /rɪsk pulɪŋ/

GENERAL

NOUN **Risk pooling** is the practice of sharing all risks among a group of insurance companies.

○ *With risk pooling arrangements, instead of participants transferring risk to someone else, each company reduces their own risk.*

○ *Risk pooling allows an insurance carrier to provide an income stream via an immediate annuity, even with its costs and expenses, far more cheaply than a person could on his or her own.*

---

run-off /rʌn ɔf/

GENERAL

NOUN If an insurance company is **in run-off**, it no longer takes on new business but still meets its liabilities to existing policyholders.

○ *The company will elect whether the termination will be on a run-off basis or a clean-cut basis with an immediate settlement of all present and future obligations under this agreement.*

○ *This once large reinsurer ceased operations last year, and is now in run-off.*

▶ COLLOCATION:
in run-off

Ss

---

safe|ty belt /ˈseɪfti bɛlt/ (safety belts)

NOUN A **safety belt** is a strap attached to the seat of a car or airplane which you fasten around your body to stop you from being thrown forward if there is an accident.

○ *The company may deny or reduce an award if the board finds the victim was not wearing protective equipment such as a safety belt.*

○ *Children must be protected in an appropriate child restraint or booster seat rather than in a safety belt at least up to the age of 8 years.*

---

safe|ty de|vice /ˈseɪfti dɪvaɪs/ (safety devices)

NOUN A **safety device** is a piece of equipment such as a fire extinguisher, safety belt, or burglar alarm that reduces loss or damage from a fire, accident, or break-in.

○ *If your house is fitted with a safety device such as a burglar alarm or smoke detector, tell your insurance company, since you can save money on your premiums.*

○ *The defective condition of the safety device in the stove was the likely cause of the fire.*

---

sal|vage¹ /ˈsælvɪdʒ/

NOUN **Salvage** is the act of taking part in a successful rescue operation to save life or property at sea, or the money payable to someone who does this.

○ *The contract defines salvage as the preservation by a voluntary salvor of a ship, cargo, and certain other classes of property at sea or in other waters from danger.*

○ *A marine casualty that requires salvage services is an emergency.*

sal|vage² /sælvɪdʒ/

COMMERCIAL INSURANCE

NOUN **Salvage** is the amount of money received by an insurer from the sale of damaged property on which a total loss has been paid to the insured.

○ *The overall loss on property after severe damage by fire or other peril is reduced by the salvage value.*

○ *Insurers receive salvage rights over property on which they have paid claims, such as badly damaged cars.*

sched|ule /skɛdʒul/ (**schedules**)

GENERAL

NOUN A **schedule** is a list of individual items covered by an insurance policy with their descriptions and values.

○ *Coverage is for damage to covered property caused by an accident to an object identified in the policy's schedule.*

○ *A vehicle schedule is a list of vehicles attached to and covered by an insurance policy.*

se|cond-hand en|dow|ment /sɛkənd hænd ɪndaʊmənt/ (**second-hand endowments**)

LIFE INSURANCE

NOUN A **second-hand endowment** is a traditional with-profits endowment policy that has been sold to a new owner part way through its term.

○ *The second-hand endowment market enables investors to buy unwanted endowment policies for more than the surrender value offered by the insurance company.*

○ *Investors will pay more than the surrender value for a second-hand endowment because the policy has greater value if it is kept in force than if it is terminated early.*

self-in|sur|ance /sɛlf ɪnʃʊərəns/

GENERAL

NOUN **Self-insurance** is the practice of insuring yourself or your property by saving your income or other funds rather than by buying an insurance policy.

- ○ *The commercial insurance market pays for losses above the specified self-insurance limit per loss, thereby stopping the cost of losses to the self-insured above the retained values.*
- ○ *Large commercial concerns may opt for self-insurance on the grounds that they are avoiding the extra expenses of an insurance policy and have sufficiently strong finances to cope with their likely losses.*

---

ser|vice in|dus|try /sɜːrvɪs ɪndəstri/ (**service industries**)

GENERAL

NOUN A **service industry** is an area of business such as banking or insurance that provides a service but does not produce anything.

- ○ *By its very character, the attention of a service industry such as insurance has primarily to be centered on marketing and customer service.*
- ○ *Insurance is a service industry where help, guidance, and advice is of paramount importance from the point of sale through to claims.*

---

set|tle a claim /sɛtᵊl ə kleɪm/ (**settles a claim, settled a claim, settling a claim**)

CLAIMS

PHRASE If an insurer **settles a claim** it pays money to a policyholder for the occurrence of a loss or risk against which they were insured.

- ○ *Insurance companies use the premiums they receive not only to settle claims but also to generate additional income and profit by investing their funds in financial securities.*
- ○ *If your car is damaged because of another driver's negligence and you ask us to settle the claim for damage to your vehicle, we will seek to recover your deductible and our payments from the other party.*

---

se|vere /sɪvɪər/

GENERAL

ADJECTIVE **Severe** injuries, damage, or illnesses are very bad or very serious.

- ○ *The program will ensure that a minimum level of coverage to meet severe healthcare needs is available to every citizen.*
- ○ *Without knowing how severe the property damage and bodily injury was, it is impossible to say how large the payout will be.*

se|ver|i|ty /sɪvɛrɪti/

SALES AND DISTRIBUTION

GENERAL

NOUN The **severity** of an injury, damage, or illness is how bad or serious it is.

○ *The value of your claim depends on the severity of your injury and the damages, such as medical expenses and lost wages.*

○ *High claims costs are generally attributable to vehicles that have a performance history resulting in a higher severity of bodily injury losses in an accident.*

> **WORD BUILDER**
> **-ity** = state or quality
>
> The suffix **-ity** is often added to adjectives to form nouns connected with a state or quality: **eligibility**, **insurability**, **liability**, **maturity**, **portability**, **severity**.

shop a|round /ʃɒp əraʊnd/ (**shops around, shopped around, shopping around**)

SALES AND DISTRIBUTION

VERB If you **shop around**, you compare the price and quality of different items or services before you decide which to buy.

○ *Once you know what your personal needs are, shop around for the best possible term life insurance quotes.*

○ *Premiums and account fees can vary, so be sure to shop around.*

short-tail busi|ness /ʃɔrt teɪl bɪznɪs/

GENERAL

NOUN **Short-tail business** is insurance business where it is known that claims will be made and settled quickly.

○ *As a true measure of loss and premium results, calendar year statistics, even for short-tail business, can be highly misleading.*

○ *Short-tail business includes most classes of property business, in which claims are reported and settled in a relatively short period of time.*

sin|gle life an|nu|i|ty /sɪŋɡəl laɪf ənuɪti/ (single life annuities)

[LIFE INSURANCE]

NOUN A **single life annuity** is an annuity where only one life is covered.

- A single life annuity guarantees a lifetime income for you alone.
- If your spouse has enough retirement income, it would pay you to select a single life annuity.

> **RELATED WORDS**
>
> Compare this with a **joint-life annuity**, which is a life insurance policy that pays a benefit that continues throughout the joint lifetime of two people until one of them dies.

sin|gle pre|mi|um /sɪŋɡəl priːmiəm/ (single premiums)

[LIFE INSURANCE]

NOUN A **single premium** is a premium that is paid in one lump sum rather than regularly in installments.

- With a single premium or immediate annuity, the annuitant pays for the annuity with a single lump sum.
- Our life insurance policy can be paid for in advance by one single premium rather than in periodic premiums.

sin|gle pre|mi|um in|sur|ance /sɪŋɡəl priːmiəm ɪnʃʊərəns/

[LIFE INSURANCE]

NOUN **Single premium insurance** is insurance where all the premium is paid at once, in one payment.

- With single premium insurance, the policyholder pays a premium just once and enjoys its benefits throughout the policy term.
- If you opt for single premium insurance, the premium is payable upfront as a lump sum.

spouse /spaʊs/ (spouses)

[LIFE INSURANCE]

NOUN Your **spouse** is your husband or wife.

○ *The insured persons in property and casualty policies may include residents of the insured's household, such as spouse and children.*

○ *If your spouse is significantly younger than you, the payout for a joint survivorship policy is significantly less than for an individual annuity.*

---

stand|ard an|nu|i|ty /stændərd ənuɪti/ (**standard annuities**)

LIFE INSURANCE: PENSIONS

NOUN A **standard annuity** is a retirement investment insurance contract that pays a regular income in return for a lump sum payment.

○ *If poor health is expected to reduce your life span, then you might qualify for an enhanced annuity, which will pay you a much higher income than a standard annuity could offer.*

○ *A standard annuity is an arrangement where you make a lump sum investment and, from this investment, you receive a guaranteed level of income.*

---

stop loss re|in|sur|ance (ABBR **SLR**) /stɒp lɒs riɪnʃʊərəns/

REINSURANCE

NOUN **Stop loss reinsurance** is a form of reinsurance under which the reinsurer pays the cedant's losses in any year over a particular percentage of the earned premium.

○ *Specific annual stop loss reinsurance limits the primary carrier's liability each year to a specified percentage of total ultimate incurred loss.*

○ *With stop loss reinsurance, the part paid by the reinsurer is not determined by the aggregate claims of the individual policy, only by the aggregate claims of the whole portfolio.*

S

---

sub|ro|ga|tion /sʌbrəgeɪʃᵊn/

CLAIMS

NOUN **Subrogation** is the right of an insurer to recover any claim payments by taking any actions against third parties, in place of the insured.

○ *A basic principle of property liability insurance contracts is the principle of subrogation, under which the insurer may be entitled to recovery from liable third parties.*

○ *The principle of subrogation was established to avoid people taking legal action against another party.*

sub|sid|ence /sʌbsɪdəns/

NOUN **Subsidence** is the process by which an area of land sinks to a lower level than the land surrounding it, or a building begins to sink into the ground.

○ *Under certain circumstances, land subsidence is covered under flood policies.*

○ *You are covered for losses from land subsidence resulting from erosion that is specifically covered under our definition of flooding.*

sum as|sured /sʌm əʃʊərd/ (**sums assured**)

NOUN The **sum assured** is the amount payable on the occurrence of an event insured against under a benefit policy, such as the death of the insured.

○ *At maturity, the endowment policy should repay the loan; if the borrower dies before maturity, the sum assured will repay the loan.*

○ *In the event of your unfortunate death due to an accident your family will receive 100 percent of the sum assured.*

sum in|sured /sʌm ɪnʃʊərd/ (**sums insured**)

NOUN The **sum insured** is the insurer's limit of liability under an insurance contract.

○ *With an increasing term contract, the sum insured increases each year by a fixed percentage.*

○ *The schedule contains the name of the insured, the sum insured, premiums payable, and any exclusions or variations that apply to the policy.*

sup|ple|men|ta|ry in|sur|ance /sʌplɪmɛntəri ɪnʃʊərəns/

NOUN **Supplementary insurance** is insurance coverage that is purchased in addition to an insurance policy to provide additional benefits or coverage.

○ *Beyond this base benefit, individuals can elect to purchase supplementary insurance to cover services not included in the package.*

○ *If you want additional protection, it makes more sense to add supplementary insurance to an extended homeowner's policy.*

sur|plus re|in|sur|ance /sɜːplʌs riːɪnʃʊərəns/

REINSURANCE

NOUN **Surplus reinsurance** is reinsurance of amounts over a specified amount of insurance.

○ *Surplus reinsurance is a form of proportional reinsurance in which risks are reinsured above a specified amount.*

○ *Surplus reinsurance requires an insurer to transfer and the reinsurer to accept the part of every risk that exceeds the insurer's predetermined retention limit.*

sur|ren|der¹ /sərɛndər/ (**surrenders, surrendered, surrendering**)

LIFE INSURANCE

VERB If you **surrender** an endowment or other life policy, you terminate it before the agreed maturity date.

○ *A fee is charged to a policyholder when a life insurance policy or annuity is surrendered for its cash value.*

○ *If the policy is surrendered before maturity, the insurance company then pays the policyholder the current cash value.*

sur|ren|der² /sərɛndər/

LIFE INSURANCE

NOUN The **surrender** of an endowment or other life policy is the situation when the policyholder decides to terminate it before its maturity date in return for a fee.

○ *Policy proceeds will be paid on a life insurance policy at death or when the insured receives payment at surrender or maturity.*

○ *The total policy loan plus unpaid interest will be subtracted from policy proceeds if the loan is outstanding at the time of death or surrender of the policy.*

sur|ren|der val|ue /sərɛndər vælyu/ (**surrender values**)

LIFE INSURANCE

NOUN The **surrender value** of a life insurance policy is the amount of money you receive if you decide that you no longer wish to continue with the policy.

○ *The policy owner has a right to terminate policy coverage in exchange for the policy's cash surrender value.*

○ *Generally speaking, the surrender value will equal cash values after a certain period of time depending on how long the policy has been in force before the policy is surrendered.*

---

sur|vive /sərvaɪv/ (survives, survived, surviving)

LIFE INSURANCE

VERB If you **survive**, you continue to live.

○ *If the insured dies within the period specified, the policy is paid to the beneficiary, and if the insured survives within the period, the contract is terminated.*

○ *With term life insurance, no benefit is payable if the insured survives past the end of the term.*

---

sur|viv|ing /sərvaɪvɪŋ/

LIFE INSURANCE

ADJECTIVE A **surviving** family member or spouse is someone who continues to live after the policyholder has died.

○ *A surviving spouse receives annual compensation equal to 50 percent of the worker's last annual rate of pay.*

○ *The death of one spouse will not trigger income taxes provided that the beneficiary was the surviving spouse.*

---

syn|di|cate /sɪndɪkɪt/ (syndicates)

UNDERWRITING

NOUN A **syndicate** is a grouping of underwriters who join together to insure very high valued property.

○ *Lloyd's of London is an insurance market organized into syndicates.*

○ *The underwriters on the floor of Lloyd's are known as lead underwriters because they lead a syndicate of underwriters.*

S

Tt

---

take out in|sur|ance /teɪk aʊt ɪnʃʊərəns/ (takes out insurance, took out insurance, taken out insurance, taking out insurance)

GENERAL

PHRASE If you **take out insurance**, you purchase coverage from an insurance company.

- ○ In some countries buyers must use domestic insurers for compulsory coverages, but are free to take out insurance from foreign insurers when coverage is not available from domestic insurers.

- ○ If the life insured commences smoking after taking out insurance at non-smoker rates, they may have an obligation to inform the insurance company who will then apply the applicable smoker rates.

---

tech|ni|cal re|serves /tɛknɪkəl rɪzɜrvz/

UNDERWRITING

NOUN **Technical reserves** are amounts of money set aside to pay for underwriting liabilities.

- ○ Insurance companies in the EU must maintain sufficient assets as technical reserves to cover all underwriting liabilities.

- ○ An insurer must calculate technical reserves for each insurance contract or contract group separately.

---

ten|ant /tɛnənt/ (tenants)

RESIDENCE INSURANCE

NOUN A **tenant** is someone who lives in a house or room and pays rent to the person who owns it.

- ○ Accidental damage covers damage caused to a property by a tenant, which does not occur as a result of normal wear and tear.

t

○ *Rent insurance covers a landlord if a fire or other insured event makes it impossible to collect rent from a tenant until the building has been replaced or repaired.*

---

ter|mi|nal ill|ness /tɜrmɪnəl ɪlnɪs/ (**terminal illnesses**)

MEDICAL INSURANCE

NOUN A **terminal illness** cannot be cured, and causes death.

○ *Life insurance could pay out a lump sum if you die or are diagnosed with a terminal illness.*

○ *A rider to the life insurance policy allows for the early payment of some portion of the policy's face amount should the insured suffer from a terminal illness.*

---

term in|sur|ance /tɜrm ɪnʃʊərəns/

LIFE INSURANCE

NOUN **Term insurance** is a type of life insurance which is paid only if the person dies within a particular period of time.

○ *Because permanent life insurance programs are designed to be permanent and pay a death benefit, the cost of insurance is considerably higher than term insurance.*

○ *Unlike term insurance, whole life insurance provides insurance coverage for the lifetime of the insured.*

---

terms and con|di|tions /tɜrmz ənd kəndɪʃənz/

GENERAL

NOUN The **terms and conditions** of your insurance coverage are the rules that govern it as defined by the insurer.

○ *Insurance is highly competitive, so if you are not happy with the terms and conditions offered by a policy, shop around.*

○ *The terms and conditions of coverage are determined by the limit of insurance chosen by the policyholder.*

---

theft /θɛft/

RESIDENCE INSURANCE

NOUN **Theft** is the crime of stealing items belonging to another person.

○ *Policies are often sold with the cellphones themselves to cover them for damage or theft.*

○ *Previously there were disputes under theft policies as to whether property mysteriously lost had or had not been stolen.*

---

third par|ty /θɜrd pɑrti/ (third parties)

NOUN A **third party** is a person claiming against an insured; the first party being the insurer and the second party being the insured.

○ *Liability insurance covers the legal liability of the insured resulting from injuries to a third party, to their body, or damage to their property.*

○ *Liability insurance offers specific protection against third party insurance claims in which payment is not made to the insured, but rather to someone suffering loss who is not a party to the insurance contract.*

---

third par|ty li|a|bil|i|ty /θɜrd pɑrti laɪəbɪlɪti/

NOUN **Third party liability** is insurance against money which an insured may have to pay to third parties if they accidentally cause them injury, loss, or damage.

○ *Travel agencies must carry third party liability coverage against damage caused to their customers and service providers.*

○ *Organizations offering holidays for unaccompanied children must have third party liability insurance against accident or injury occurring during their trip.*

> **RELATED WORDS**
>
> Compare this with **comprehensive** insurance, which provides protection against most risks, including third-party liability, fire, theft, and damage.

t

---

ton|tine /tɒntin/ (tontines)

NOUN A **tontine** is a system of mutual life insurance where benefits are received by those participants who survive and keep their policies throughout a stated period.

○ *Under a tontine, the government paid interest on money raised and the total amount accumulated was divided among the surviving members of the group at a predetermined date.*

○ *Tontine life insurance policies provide benefits only to survivors who live to the end of a certain period of time.*

> **WORD ORIGINS**
>
> This word comes from the name of a 17th century Italian banker, Lorenzo Tonti.

---

tor|na|do /tɔrneɪdoʊ/ (tornadoes)

RESIDENCE INSURANCE

NOUN A **tornado** is a violent wind storm consisting of a tall column of air that spins around very fast and causes a lot of damage.

○ *They filed their claim, stating that their home was leveled by hurricane-force winds, which caused a tornado, which was followed by flooding.*

○ *The storms produced tornadoes, which caused damage to both automobiles and homes.*

> **EVENTS THAT CAUSE DAMAGE TO PROPERTY**
>
> earthquake, flood, landslide, subsidence, tornado, tsunami

---

to|tal loss /toʊtᵊl lɔs/ (total losses)

CLAIMS

NOUN A **total loss** is a situation in which an insured item is totally lost, destroyed, or damaged, and no money can be recovered.

○ *A vehicle is considered a total loss if it cannot be repaired safely, or if repairing the vehicle is not economically practical.*

○ *You may wish to insure at 100 percent of replacement cost so you will have sufficient coverage in the event of total loss.*

---

to|tal prob|a|ble loss /toʊtᵊl prɒbəbᵊl lɔs/ (total probable losses)

UNDERWRITING

NOUN A **total probable loss** is the highest degree of loss or damage that is probable if an insured event occurs.

○ *Insurance for losses higher than $25,000 and up to $3,000,000 is unnecessary because the maximum total probable loss is only about $250,000.*

○ *If the amount insured is less than the full value of the property insured, this produces an inadequate premium not based on total probable loss.*

---

track|er fund /trǽkər fʌnd/ (**tracker funds**)

LIFE INSURANCE: PENSIONS

NOUN A **tracker fund** is an investment in which stocks in different companies are bought and sold so that the value of the stocks held always matches the average value of stocks in a stock market.

○ *An index tracker fund is a collective investment vehicle that is designed to follow the performance of a particular index.*

○ *A tracker fund aims to shadow the performance of a specified stock market index.*

---

trad|ed en|dow|ment /tréɪdɪd ɪndáʊmənt/ (**traded endowments**)

LIFE INSURANCE

NOUN A **traded endowment** is a traditional with-profits endowment policy that has been sold to a new owner part way through its term.

○ *A traded endowment policy has been sold by the original policyholder to an investor before the policy matures.*

○ *Endowment policies traditionally levy all their charges in the first few years, but you can avoid these charges by buying a traded endowment policy, where the original policyholder sells it at auction.*

---

tra|di|tion|al pol|i|cy /trədɪ́ʃənᵊl pɒ́lɪsi/ (**traditional policies**)

LIFE INSURANCE

NOUN A **traditional policy** is a life insurance policy in which the policyholder pays premiums into a general fund and benefits are calculated using statistics.

○ *A universal life policy generally earns interest at a higher rate than a traditional policy.*

○ *For the traditional policy the basic sum assured is taken as the sum of the premiums payable.*

trail com|mis|sion /treɪl kəmɪʃⁿn/

SALES AND DISTRIBUTION

NOUN A **trail commission** is a further commission of between 0.1 and 1 percent that is paid to an advisor provided that the client's funds remain invested in the product for a specified time.

○ Mortgage brokers are paid an ongoing trail commission that is on average 0.18 percent of the loan amount per annum paid monthly.

○ Advisors may also get trail commission, usually 0.5 percent of your fund, for every year you hold the investment.

trav|el in|sur|ance /trævⁿl ɪnʃʊərəns/

GENERAL

NOUN **Travel insurance** is insurance coverage for risks associated with traveling such as loss of luggage, delays, and death or injury while in a foreign country.

○ In cases of overseas hospitalizations and deaths where victims are not covered by travel insurance, such personal tragedies are further compounded by a long-term financial burden.

○ You may find that your home contents insurance covers your possessions outside the home, including abroad, so you can adjust your travel insurance policy and potentially pay lower premiums.

trea|ty /triːti/ (treaties)

REINSURANCE

NOUN A **treaty** is a contract that provides for a number of reinsurances over a period of time.

○ Under a treaty each party automatically accepts specific percentages of the insurer's business.

○ A reinsurance treaty is an agreement between a reinsurer and a ceding insurer setting forth details of the reinsurance arrangement.

trust /trʌst/ (trusts)

LIFE INSURANCE: PENSIONS

NOUN A **trust** is an organization or group that has control over money that will be used to help someone else.

○ If you set up a trust before your death, after your death property can be quickly and quietly distributed to the beneficiaries.

○ A life insurance trust is a type of life insurance policy where a company is named as the beneficiary and distributes the proceeds of the policy under the terms of the agreement.

---

trus|tee /trʌstiː/ (trustees)

LIFE INSURANCE: PENSIONS

NOUN A **trustee** is a person who has control of money or property that is in a trust for someone else.

○ Either on the death of the life assured or on maturity of the policy, the insurance company will have to make the payment to the trustees appointed.

○ The trustee has legal ownership of the trust property, and is required by law to manage and distribute it in accordance with the instructions specified in the trust agreement.

> **WORD BUILDER**
> **-ee** = person
>
> The suffix **-ee** is added to verbs to form nouns meaning people who are doing a particular thing or are in a particular state: **retiree**, **trustee**.

---

tsu|na|mi /tsʊnɑːmi/ (tsunamis)

RESIDENCE INSURANCE

NOUN A **tsunami** is a very large wave, often caused by an earthquake, that flows onto the land and can cause widespread deaths and destruction.

○ Although the policy will cover small-scale water damage from a leaky roof or bad plumbing, for example, it won't cover larger-scale water damage like flooding during a serious storm or tsunami.

○ Local tsunami hazard and risk is high, as earthquakes are common in the area.

Uu

um|brel|la pol|i|cy /ʌmbrɛlə pɒlɪsi/ (**umbrella policies**)

NOUN An **umbrella policy** is a policy that provides excess limits and gives additional excess coverage over the normal limits and coverage of liability policies.

○ *The umbrella policy fills gaps in coverage under basic liability policies.*

○ *You may purchase higher limits of liability inexpensively under a personal umbrella policy.*

---

un|der|in|sured /ʌndərɪnʃʊərd/

ADJECTIVE If you are **underinsured**, you do not have enough insurance.

○ *An underinsured policyholder may only receive part of the cost of replacing or repairing damaged items.*

○ *If the policyholder is underinsured, he pays a proportion of the loss himself.*

---

un|der|write /ʌndərraɪt/ (**underwrites, underwrote, underwritten, underwriting**)

VERB If an insurer **underwrites** an insurance policy or a risk, they accept liability if particular losses occur.

○ *The physician's statement provides the insurance company with information relevant to underwriting a risk or settling a claim.*

○ *Insurers underwrite policies knowing and accepting the possibility of a limit loss.*

un|der|writ|er /ˈʌndərraɪtər/ (underwriters)

UNDERWRITING

NOUN An **underwriter** is a person or business that underwrites insurance policies.

○ *The ability to separately evaluate each risk reinsured increases the probability that the underwriter can price the contract to more accurately reflect the risks involved.*

○ *The underwriter is the individual responsible for reviewing applications and medical histories and assessing the applicant's risk to the insurance company.*

un|der|writ|ing /ˈʌndərraɪtɪŋ/

UNDERWRITING

NOUN **Underwriting** is the acceptance of insurance business by an underwriter.

○ *Underwriting on a high-risk applicant indicates that an extra premium is required to cover additional risks, such as smoking.*

○ *Underwriting is the process of selecting risks for insurance and determining in what amounts and on what terms the insurance company will accept the risk.*

un|em|ploy|ment in|sur|ance /ˈʌnɪmplɔɪmənt ɪnʃʊərəns/

GENERAL

NOUN **Unemployment insurance** is a system that makes payments to people if they lose their jobs.

○ *Any employee who loses their job as specified in the scheme will be entitled to a monthly unemployment insurance benefit for a specified period.*

○ *Mortgage unemployment insurance pays the mortgage of a policyholder who becomes involuntarily unemployed.*

WORD BUILDER

un- = not

The prefix **un-** is often added to adjectives to make their opposites:
unemployment, **uninsurable**, **uninsured**.

---

u

un|in|sur|a|ble /ʌnɪnʃʊərəbᵊl/

GENERAL

ADJECTIVE An **uninsurable** risk or person is not eligible for insurance.

○ Someone in poor health will have to pay a very high premium, or even be uninsurable.

○ For applications on property that may be uninsurable, coverage cannot begin until after an inspection is completed.

un|in|sured /ʌnɪnʃʊərd/

GENERAL

ADJECTIVE If you are **uninsured**, you are not covered for a risk.

○ He incurred over $1 million in medical bills arising from an auto accident with an uninsured motorist.

○ People who are uninsured include people who have low incomes, people who have costly preexisting health conditions, and those whose employers do not offer group health insurance.

up|front /ʌpfrʌnt/

SALES AND DISTRIBUTION

ADJECTIVE An **upfront** expense or payment is charged or paid in advance.

○ Annuities are policies that pay a regular benefit as long as the insured person is alive, in return for an upfront single premium.

○ With this policy, your insurer will give you an upfront payment and will then wait for the other motorist to pay them, so that you won't have to.

ut|most good faith (also known as **uberrima fides**) /ʌtmoʊst gʊd feɪθ/

GENERAL

NOUN **Utmost good faith** is a principle used in insurance contracts that legally obliges all parties to reveal to the others all important information.

○ Insurance contracts are agreements made in the utmost good faith, which implies a standard of honesty greater than that usually required in most ordinary commercial contracts.

○ The policy is voidable if utmost good faith is not observed by both parties.

Vv

---

val|ued pol|i|cy /ˈvælyud ˈpɒlɪsi/ (valued policies)

GENERAL

NOUN A **valued policy** is an insurance policy in which the amount payable for a claim is agreed upon when the policy is issued, and is not related to the actual value of a loss.

○ With a valued policy, the insurer pays a specified amount of money to or on behalf of the insured upon the occurrence of a defined loss.

○ A valued policy pays a specified sum not related in any way to the extent of the loss.

---

var|i|a|ble u|ni|ver|sal life in|sur|ance (ABBR VUL)
/ˈvɛəriəbəl ˌyunɪˈvɜrsəl laɪf ɪnˈʃʊərəns/

LIFE INSURANCE

NOUN **Variable universal life insurance** is a type of life insurance that allows you to invest the cash value in a wide variety of separate accounts.

○ A variable universal life insurance policy provides for life insurance, the amount or duration of which varies according to the investment experience of any separate account or accounts.

○ When you buy a variable universal life insurance policy, you allocate your premium payments to a separate account, which is made up of variable sub-accounts.

---

ve|hi|cle /ˈviːɪkəl/ (vehicles)

VEHICLE INSURANCE

NOUN A **vehicle** is a machine with an engine, such as a bus, car, or truck, that carries people or things from place to place.

○ In order to operate a motor vehicle legally, a driver must obtain a minimum level of auto insurance to satisfy the laws of the road.

○ *In the United States, if you are caught driving without insurance your license could be suspended and your vehicle impounded.*

---

ve|hi|cle in|sur|ance /vˈiːkəl ɪnʃʊərəns/

VEHICLE INSURANCE

NOUN **Vehicle insurance** is insurance purchased for cars, trucks, motorcycles, and other road vehicles.

○ *In many jurisdictions it is compulsory to have vehicle insurance before using or keeping a motor vehicle on public roads.*

○ *Vehicle insurance would typically cover both the property risk (theft or damage to the vehicle) and the liability risk (legal claims arising from an accident).*

> **VEHICLE INSURANCE**
>
> The following are types of vehicle insurance:
> collision coverage, collision damage waiver, GAP insurance, no-fault insurance
>
> The following are discounts for vehicle insurance:
> accident-free discount, good driver discount

---

vi|at|i|cal set|tle|ment /vaɪˈætɪkəl sˈɛtəlmənt/ (**viatical settlements**)

LIFE INSURANCE

NOUN In a **viatical settlement**, a third party buys a life insurance policy owned by a person with only a short time to live, so that the person can use the proceeds during their lifetime.

○ *In a viatical settlement, a terminally ill policyholder sells their life insurance policy and names the buyer as beneficiary and owner.*

○ *A viatical settlement involves the purchase of a life insurance policy from an elderly or terminally ill policyholder.*

> **WORD ORIGINS**
>
> This term comes from the word "Viaticum," which is the communion given, especially in the Roman Catholic church, to a person who is on the point of death. Viaticum is a Latin word meaning "provisions for a journey."

vi|sion care /vɪʒ°n keər/

MEDICAL INSURANCE

NOUN **Vision care** is the care and treatment of eyes, eyesight conditions, and vision.

○ Vision care coverage provides benefits for expenses the insured incurs in obtaining eye examinations and corrective lenses.

○ Eye surgery to correct vision is frequently covered under vision care insurance.

void /vɔɪd/

GENERAL

ADJECTIVE If a contract or official agreement is **void**, it is not legal and has no effect.

○ If the voyage itself is illegal under the laws of the country under whose flag the ship sails, then the insurance is void.

○ The policy is void if the policyholder, at any time, intentionally conceals or misrepresents a material fact.

V

Ww

---

wait|ing pe|ri|od /weɪtɪŋ pɪəriəd/ (**waiting periods**)

LIFE INSURANCE

NOUN A **waiting period** is a period of time after insurance coverage has been bought during which no claims can be made.

- ○ *Most insurance companies will provide coverage for diseases caused by diabetes and hypertension only after a waiting period of 3–5 years.*
- ○ *The employee is covered from day one under the policy, without any waiting period.*

---

waiv|er of pre|mi|um /weɪvər əv prɪmiəm/ (**waivers of premium**)

MEDICAL INSURANCE

NOUN A **waiver of premium** is a provision that allows the insured not to pay premiums during a period of disability that has lasted for a particular length of time.

- ○ *The waiver of premium for disability remains in effect as long as the insured is disabled.*
- ○ *Under the waiver of premium provision, the insurance carrier will waive premium payments for you after you have been totally disabled for at least six months.*

---

whole life in|sur|ance /hoʊl laɪf ɪnʃʊərəns/

LIFE INSURANCE

NOUN **Whole life insurance** is a life insurance policy that continues for the insured's whole life and requires premiums to be paid every year into the policy.

- ○ *Some term policies are convertible to whole life insurance at any time without evidence of insurability.*

○ *Whole life insurance is permanent level insurance protection for the whole of life, from policy issue to the death of the insured.*

---

wid|ow /wɪdoʊ/ (**widows**)

LIFE INSURANCE

NOUN A **widow** is a woman whose husband has died and who has not married again.

○ *Attach a copy of the employee's death certificate and a copy of the certificate of the marriage to the widow or widower.*

○ *A funeral advancement option allows the widow or widower of the deceased policyholder to get a portion of the benefit upfront for the funeral expenses.*

---

wid|ow|er /wɪdoʊər/ (**widowers**)

LIFE INSURANCE

NOUN A **widower** is a man whose wife has died and who has not married again.

○ *Remarriage renders a surviving widow or widower ineligible for this benefit.*

○ *If you are a widow or widower of an individual who died as an employee or retiree, your survivor annuity begins on the day after the employee's or retiree's death.*

---

will /wɪl/ (**wills**)

LIFE INSURANCE

NOUN A **will** is a legal document in which you declare what you want to happen to your money and property when you die.

○ *The estate is distributed to heirs according to the terms of the person's will.*

○ *A will distributes solely-owned property of a deceased that is left over after paying creditors and taxes.*

TALKING ABOUT WILLS

When you **make** a will, you **bequeath** your possessions to others.

If your will **stipulates** something, it says that something must happen.

W

work|ers' com|pen|sa|tion /wɜrkərz kɒmpənseɪʃ°n/

LIFE INSURANCE

NOUN **Workers' compensation** is insurance in the U.S. that replaces wages and pays for medical treatment for employees who are injured while they are working.

○ *To protect injured employees, state laws set out requirements for the assumption of workers' compensation programs.*

○ *Workers' compensation provides benefits for injury, disability, or death as a result of an occupational hazard.*

---

write cov|er /raɪt kʌvər/ (writes cover, wrote cover, written cover, writing cover)

UNDERWRITING

PHRASE If an insurance company **writes cover**, it underwrites a risk or insures someone.

○ *German insurers tend to issue ten-year policies, whereas Lloyd's syndicates write cover on an annual basis.*

○ *It is normal for a ship to be surveyed in order for insurance companies to establish seaworthiness before they write cover.*

---

write off /raɪt ɔf/ (writes off, wrote off, written off, writing off)

VEHICLE INSURANCE

VERB If you **write off** a vehicle, you damage it so badly that it can never be used again, or you declare that this has happened.

○ *If a policyholder has a car accident and the car is written off, they will receive a check for the value of the car at the time of claim.*

○ *My car has been recovered since being stolen, but it has been written off.*

---

write-off /raɪt ɔf/

VEHICLE INSURANCE

NOUN A **write-off** is a vehicle that has been so badly damaged that it can never be used again.

○ *If your car is declared to be a write-off, the insurance company will deduct the excess agreed on the policy from the settlement payment it makes to you.*

○ *My mechanic has already indicated that the car might be a write-off since repairing the damage will cost more than the car is worth.*

W

Practice and Solutions

1. Match the two parts together.

1 An adjusted claim

2 A fraudulent act or insurance claim

3 A mature bond or life insurance policy

4 Reviewable premiums or payments

5 If a contract or official agreement is void,

6 Noncontributory insurance

a is ready to be paid.

b it is not legal and has no effect.

c are not guaranteed and may be increased or decreased.

d is insurance that is completely paid for by the company, not the employee.

e has been evaluated by a loss adjuster.

f is deliberately deceitful, dishonest, or untrue.

2. For each question, choose the correct answer.

a beneficiary	an actuary	a loss adjuster

1 A mathematician who uses statistics to calculate premiums, dividends, etc. is called ....

an underwriter	an appraiser	a risk manager

2 A person who decides whether or not to accept liability if particular losses occur on an insurance policy or risk is called

....

a loss adjuster	an underwriter	a risk manager

3 Someone whose job is to prevent or reduce the likelihood that dangerous accidents or mistakes will occur, or to reduce the amount of money lost by the insurance company is called ....

> **an actuary**   **a financial adviser**   **an appraiser**

4 An expert in the valuation of certain types of property, who provides expert advice to insurance loss adjusters is called

....

> **a loss adjuster**   **a risk manager**   **an appraiser**

5 A person who is employed by an insurance company to evaluate an insurance claim and decide how much money should be paid to a person making a claim is called ....

> **a risk manager**   **a financial adviser**   **an underwriter**

6 A life insurance and investment specialist who tells you how best to invest your money and protect your and your family's future is called

....

3. Find the words or phrases that do not belong.

1 Types of ratio ....
   a claims ratio **b** noncontributory ratio **c** combined ratio
   d loss ratio

2 Types of insurance ....
   a accident insurance **b** fleet insurance **c** growth insurance
   d aviation insurance

3 Types of policy ....
   a inflation policy **b** all-risk policy **c** endowment policy
   d umbrella policy

4 Types of annuity ....
   a deferred annuity **b** claimed annuity **c** immediate annuity
   d standard annuity

5 Types of premium ....

   a gross premium **b** regular premium **c** single premium

   d double premium

6 Types of loss ....

   a consequential loss **b** estimated maximum loss **c** likely minimum loss **d** total probable loss

4. Choose the correct word or phrase to fill each gap.

> **an equity-linked policy**   **a first-loss policy**
> **an endowment policy**

1 An insurance policy that provides life coverage, but that pays a sum of money if the policyholder is still alive after an agreed period of time is called ....

> **an annuitant**   **an appraiser**   **an underwriter**

2 A person receiving an income under an annuity contract is called ....

> **surrender**   **endorsement**   **inception**

3 The date when a risk or policy started and when it started to be covered is called its ....

> **a mutual fund**   **a tracker fund**   **an investment fund**

4 An investment in which stocks in different companies are bought and sold so that the value of the stocks held always matches the average value of stocks in a stock market is called ....

commutation	coinsurance	inception

5 The formal ending of an insurance or reinsurance agreement by payment of an agreed sum in settlement is called

....

maturity value	surrender value	equivalent value

6 The amount of money you receive if you decide that you no longer wish to continue with a policy is called its ....

5. Put each sentence into the correct order.

1 wasn't too expensive / qualified for / my policy / an accident-free bonus / because I

....

....

2 including collision / damage waiver / to take out / it is advisable / comprehensive insurance

....

....

3 paralyzed from / in a / she was / hit and run / the waist down

....

....

4 on a patch / his car / of ice / and wrote off / he skidded

....

....

5 automobile insurance / at the rising / many drivers / cost of their / are alarmed

....

....

6 no-fault insurance the / under the rules / of Ontario's / paid for the repairs / driver's company

....

....

6. Which sentences are correct?

1 If an insurer settles a claim, it agrees a contract for the insurance that a client wants.   ....

2 If an insurer refuses a proposal, it does not agree to underwrite a risk for a client.   ....

3 If you calculate a premium, you decide how much a customer will have to pay for it.   ....

4 If someone draws a pension, they pay money into their pension policy.   ....

5 If you assign a policy, you transfer ownership of it to another person.   ....

6 If an insurer pools a risk, it takes on the whole of that risk.   ....

7. Complete the sentences by writing one word or phrase in each gap.

| subsidence | property | tenant |
| homeowners | depreciation | malicious damage |

1 The costs of maintenance and .... are incurred by the owners of the vehicles.

2 We arrange coverage exclusively for .... aged 55 or more.

3   They made a claim in connection with an incident of

....

4   Unless we cut down the trees, our insurers will not cover us for

....

5   You should always inform your insurer if you have a

.... in your property.

6   You must take all reasonable steps to secure your

....

8. Rearrange the letters to find words. Use the definitions to help you.

1 **viddenid**   ....
   (a sum of money from a company's net profits that is distributed to the
   holders of certain insurance policies)

2 **tynaiun**   ....
   (a contract of insurance to provide an income to the policyholder for
   a set period of time)

3 **netterirem**   ....
   (the time when you stop working, usually because of your age, or the
   period when you have stopped working)

4 **reetsut**   ....
   (a person who has control of money or property that is in a trust for
   someone else)

5 **snubo**   ....
   (a sum of money that an insurance company pays to its policyholders,
   for example a percentage of the company's profits)

6 **file narecsuin**   ....
   (insurance that pays a sum of money to you after a period of time, or to
   your family when you die)

9. Match the two parts together.

1 If you annuitize a lump sum payment,

2 If you endorse an insurance policy,

3 If you surrender an endowment or other life policy,

4 If you coinsure property,

5 If an insurer loads a premium,

6 If an insurer underwrites an insurance policy or a risk,

a you add a clause or amendment to it allowing for change of coverage.

b they increase it to cover expenses or an extra risk.

c you insure it jointly with another person or company.

d you terminate it before the agreed maturity date.

e they accept liability if particular losses occur.

f you convert it into a regular income.

10. For each question, choose the correct answer.

commission	contibution	copay

1 The amount of a medical service or prescription that a patient is responsible for, while the insurance company covers the remaining cost is called ....

an impairment	a lapse	a loss

2 A condition in which a part of a person's mind or body is damaged or is not working properly is called ....

| a cash plan | a gross written premium | an indemnity plan |

3 A healthcare plan that allows policyholders to choose any healthcare provider they wish, and charges them a fee depending on the rules of the policy is called ....

| an exclusion | a waiver of premium | a preexisting condition |

4 A provision that allows the insured not to pay premiums during a period of disability that has lasted for a particular length of time is called ....

| an inpatient | a tenant | an outpatient |

5 Someone who goes to a hospital for treatment but does not stay overnight is called ....

| deferred period | trial period | cooling-off period |

6 The period of time from when a person has become unable to work until the time that the benefit begins to be paid is called the
....

11. Put each sentence into the correct order.

1 his daughter / as the beneficiary / he had named / insurance policy / of his life

....
....

2 the pension scheme / generous / the company offers / employer contributions / includes

....
....

3 pension as a / to take / she was able / lump sum payment / part of her

....

....

4 life insurance / pension / include free / and an index-linked /
   company benefits

....

....

5 from his job in / he took / start a photography business / early
   retirement / teaching in order to

....

....

6 $40,000 when the / a monthly $66.60 premium / we were told that /
   policy matured / would turn into

....

....

12. Which sentences are correct?

1 If an insurance company accepts a risk, it knows it
   will definitely have to make a payment.   ....

2 If an insurer issues a policy, they create it and provide
   it to a customer.   ....

3 If an insurance company excludes a risk, they say that
   the policy does not cover that risk.   ....

4 If you file a claim, you agree that your claim is not valid.   ....

5 If an insurer rescinds a contact, it agrees to pay money
   to the client.   ....

6 If you manage a risk, you decide the best way to deal with it.   ....

13. Choose the correct word or phrase to fill each gap.

> **margin**   **ratio**   **debit**

1   The amount of money that an insurance company pays out in one year, divided by the amount of money that it receives in premiums is called a loss ....

> **cooling-off**   **decision**   **waiver**

2   A set time limit within which policyholders have the right to cancel an insurance policy without any penalty is called a .... period.

> **returning**   **repatriation**   **transportation**

3   The costs involved in transporting a claimant or their body back to their own country after they have been injured or killed in a foreign country are called .... expenses.

> **follower**   **linked**   **tracker**

4   An investment in which stocks in different companies are bought and sold so that the value of the stocks held always matches the average value of stocks in a stock market is called a .... fund.

> **valued**   **fixed**   **tracker**

5   An insurance policy in which the amount payable for a claim is agreed upon when the policy is issued, and is not related to the actual value of a loss is called a .... policy.

> **a fast-track**   **an end-of-year**   **an immediate**

6   An annuity contract in which payouts begin immediately or within one year is called .... annuity.

14. Put the correct word in each gap.

tornado	subsidence	flood
earthquake	tsunami	landslide

1 a sudden shaking of the earth's surface ....

2 a very large wave, often caused by an earthquake, that flows onto the land ....

3 a violent wind storm consisting of a tall column of air that spins around very fast ....

4 a large amount of earth or rocks falling down a hill, cliff, or the side of a mountain ....

5 a large amount of water covers an area which is usually dry ....

6 the process by which an area of land sinks to a lower level than the land surrounding it ....

15. Complete the sentences by writing one word or phrase in each gap.

exclusion	adverse selection	nondisclosure
endorsement	syndicate	loading

1 .... is the tendency of those in dangerous jobs or with high-risk lifestyles to want to take out life insurance.

2 An .... is a clause in or an amendment to an insurance policy allowing for change of coverage.

3 A .... is an addition to an insurance premium to cover expenses or an extra risk.

4 A .... is a grouping of underwriters who join together to insure very high value property.

5 .... is failure to inform an underwriter or insurer of all the facts relating to a life or health insurance proposal.

6 An .... is a clause in an insurance policy that excludes particular losses or risks.

16. Match the two parts together.

1 If a company or person cedes business,

a they deliberately deceive them in order to gain insurance benefits.

2 If someone defrauds an insurer,

b it is no longer valid.

3 If an insurance policy expires,

c they transfer the risk from an insurance company to a reinsurance company.

4 If an insurer reimburses a policyholder,

5 If you abandon insured property that has suffered partial loss or damage,

d you provide information about a risk that may be relevant when calculating the premium.

6 If you disclose information to an insurer,

e it pays them the expenses incurred as a loss covered by the insurance policy.

f you give it to the insurers so that a claim for a total loss may be made.

17. For each question, choose the correct answer.

| an excess   a front-end load   a back-end load |

1   A charge that an investor pays when they cancel a life insurance policy
    is called ....

| stop loss reinsurance   quota share reinsurance
proportional reinsurance |

2   The form of reinsurance under which the reinsurer pays the cedant's
    losses in any year over a particular percentage of the earned premium
    is called ....

| retrocession   subrogation   reversion |

3   The right of an insurer to recover any claim payments by taking any
    actions against third parties, in place of the insured is called

    ....

| force majeure   malicious damage   subsidence |

4   An unexpected event, such as a war or an act of God is called

    ....

| rescission   retrocession   subrogation |

5   The reinsuring of a risk by a reinsurer is called ....

| exposure   disclosure   bonding |

6   The provision of information about a risk to an insurer that may be
    relevant when calculating the premium is called

    ....

18. Put each sentence into the correct order.

1 long-term health insurance / care in her home / which meant that / my mother had / she could afford

....

....

2 scheme offers / our company / sickness and / a range of / death benefits

....

....

3 the insurer covered / of $100 / the cost of the flight / pay an excess / but we had to

....

....

4 to assess / a number of / ability to work / criteria are used / a claimant's

....

....

5 for people living / in flood areas / to provide coverage / working with insurers / the government is

....

....

6 of receiving / normally be made / payment should / a claim form / within ten days

....

....

PRACTICE PRACTICE PRACTICE PRACTICE PRACTICE PRACTICE

19. Rearrange the letters to find words. Use the definitions to help you.

1 **necuraniser** ....
(insurance protection taken out by an insurer to limit its exposure to losses on an original insurance contract)

2 **lare settae** ....
(property in the form of land, houses or other buildings)

3 **bledou medniytni** ....
(a clause in life insurance policies that provides for the payment of double the policy's face value in the event of the policyholder's accidental death)

4 **nycage** ....
(a group of people who sell and manage insurance contracts)

5 **rediwwo** ....
(a man whose wife has died and who has not married again)

6 **gearkerob** ....
(the money paid to an insurance broker)

20. Complete the sentences by writing one phrase in each gap.

Catastrophe excess of loss	Dynamic insurance
Forced place insurance	Whole life insurance
Workers' compensation	Product liability insurance

1 .... is insurance in the U.S. that replaces wages and pays for medical treatment for employees who are injured while they are working.

2 .... is a life insurance policy that continues for the insured's whole life and requires premiums to be paid every year into the policy.

3 .... is insurance for a producer or supplier of goods against injury to third parties or loss of or damage to their property that is caused by a fault in the goods.

4 .... is insurance taken out by a bank or creditor on an uninsured debtor's behalf on a property that is being used as collateral.

5 .... is a form of excess of loss reinsurance where the reinsurer agrees to reimburse the amount of a very large loss in excess of a particular sum.

6 .... is a type of insurance coverage where the policyholder can choose to increase benefits and premiums by a fixed percentage each year to offset the effects of inflation.

Solutions

Exercise 1

1. **e** has been evaluated by a loss adjuster.
2. **f** is deliberately deceitful, dishonest, or untrue.
3. **a** is ready to be paid.
4. **c** are not guaranteed and may be increased or decreased.
5. **b** it is not legal and has no effect.
6. **d** is insurance that is completely paid for by the company, not the employee.

Exercise 2

1. an actuary
2. an underwriter
3. a risk manager
4. an appraiser
5. a loss adjuster
6. a financial adviser

Exercise 3

1. **b** noncontributory ratio
2. **c** growth insurance
3. **a** inflation policy
4. **b** claimed annuity
5. **d** double premium
6. **c** likely minimum loss

Exercise 4

1. an endowment policy
2. an annuitant
3. inception
4. a tracker fund
5. commutation
6. surrender value

Exercise 5

1. my policy wasn't too expensive because I qualified for an accident-free bonus
2. it is advisable to take out comprehensive insurance including collision damage waiver
3. she was paralyzed from the waist down in a hit and run
4. he skidded on a patch of ice and wrote off his car
5. many drivers are alarmed at the rising cost of their automobile insurance
6. under the rules of Ontario's no-fault insurance the driver's company paid for the repairs

Exercise 6

2. If an insurer refuses a proposal, it does not agree to underwrite a risk for a client.
3. If you calculate a premium, you decide how much a customer will have to pay for it.
5. If you assign a policy, you transfer ownership of it to another person.

Exercise 7

1. depreciation
2. homeowners
3. malicious damage
4. subsidence
5. tenant
6. property

Exercise 8

1. dividend
2. annuity
3. retirement
4. trustee
5. bonus
6. life insurance

Exercise 9

1. **f** you convert it into a regular income.
2. **a** you add a clause or amendment to it allowing for change of coverage.
3. **d** you terminate it before the agreed maturity date.
4. **c** you insure it jointly with another person or company.
5. **b** they increase it to cover expenses or an extra risk.
6. **e** they accept liability if particular losses occur.

Exercise 10

1. copay
2. an impairment
3. an indemnity plan
4. a waiver of premium
5. an outpatient
6. deferred period

Exercise 11

1. he had named his daughter as the beneficiary of his life insurance policy

2 the pension scheme the company offers includes generous employer contributions

3 she was able to take part of her pension as a lump sum payment

4 company benefits include free life insurance and an index-linked pension

5 he took early retirement from his job in teaching in order to start a photography business

6 we were told that a monthly $66.60 premium would turn into $40,000 when the policy matured

Exercise 12

2 If an insurer issues a policy, they create it and provide it to a customer.

3 If an insurance company excludes a risk, they say that the policy does not cover that risk.

6 If you manage a risk, you decide the best way to deal with it.

Exercise 13

1 ratio
2 cooling-off
3 repatriation
4 tracker
5 valued
6 an immediate

Exercise 14

1 earthquake
2 tsunami
3 tornado
4 landslide
5 flood
6 subsidence

Exercise 15

1 adverse selection
2 endorsement
3 loading
4 syndicate
5 nondisclosure
6 exclusion

Exercise 16

1 c they transfer the risk from an insurance company to a reinsurance company.

2 a they deliberately deceive them in order to gain insurance benefits.

3 b it is no longer valid.

4 e it pays them the expenses incurred as a loss covered by the insurance policy.

5 f you give it to the insurers so that a claim for a total loss may be made.

6 d you provide information about a risk that may be relevant when calculating the premium.

Exercise 17

1 a back-end load
2 stop loss reinsurance
3 subrogation
4 force majeure
5 retrocession
6 disclosure

Exercise 18

1 my mother had long-term health insurance which meant that she could afford care in her home

2 our company scheme offers a range of sickness and death benefits

3 the insurer covered the cost of the flight but we had to pay an excess of $100

4 a number of criteria are used to assess a claimant's ability to work

5 the government is working with insurers to provide coverage for people living in flood areas

6 payment should normally be made within ten days of receiving a claim form

Exercise 19

1 reinsurance
2 real estate
3 double indemnity
4 agency
5 widower
6 brokerage

Exercise 20

1 Workers' compensation
2 Whole life insurance
3 Product liability insurance
4 Forced place insurance
5 Catastrophe excess of loss
6 Dynamic insurance

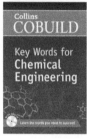
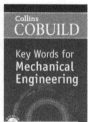

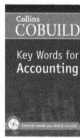

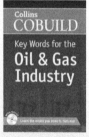